World War II, the Korean War, and the Vietnam War. Robert provides explicit and thorough details of Colonel Lippman's life and military accomplishments, woven with historical settings and context which figuratively places you in the foxhole right next to this great American hero. This book should be required reading for today's military officer corps."

—CPT Kelly Galvin, award-winning author of *PowerPoint Ranger: My Iraq War Logs*

"Rob Lofthouse has penned an inspiring biography of Lt. Colonel Gordon Lippman with both careful attention to historical facts and a great deal of compassion. He tells the story with a sense of immediacy that unveils how Lippman's actions earned Bronze and Silver Stars and other military honors. The personal memories from Lippman's family are a moving testament to help answer the question 'Where does America get such gallant men?'"

—Carol Van Den Hende, award-winning author of *Goodbye, Orchid*

"A well-written account of one hero's participation in three of our nation's wars. Lofthouse keeps the narrative flowing so that the reader is engaged in each and every battle. The details about battlefield operations are especially noteworthy. The reader will get a clear appreciation for the complexity of military war operations and the sacrifices of our men and women in uniform. Great documentation of military war history."

—George W. Kohn, Colonel, USAF (Ret), award-winning author of *Vector to Destiny: Journey of a Vietnam F-4 Fighter Pilot*

"Quite a story, and I'm very glad you're going to tell it. Thanks for giving me the chance to read it."

—Jay Franz, Lieutenant Colonel, US Army (Ret)

"Rob Lofthouse has written an authentic, moving memorial to the life of a great American and soldier. Gordon Lippman's extraordinary military service included combat tours in World War II, Korea, and finally Viet Nam, sacrificing his life for his fellow service members and a country he loved. Rob's account of Gordon's life is interwoven with America's story—and this book helps remind us that freedom isn't free. May we never forget great Americans like Gordon, his fellow soldiers, their families, and the values that inspire greatness."

—Jim Latham, Colonel, US Army (Ret)

"Rob Lofthouse takes you into the reality of a true soldier. Colossians 3:23 sets the stage for Gordon Lippman's life, and Lofthouse captures it magnificently! 'Whatever you do, work at it with all your heart, as working for the Lord, not for human masters.' Throughout WWII, the Korean War, and Vietnam, Gordon Lippmann led and cared for his men during war times and peacetime challenges. This recipient of the Distinguished Service Cross was ever present as a warrior/leader and, equally as important, as a follower who carried out the orders of his superiors. Yes, Gordon Lippman was the kind of soldier we aspire to be. I recommend this book to anyone interested in becoming a soldier leader!"

—Donald A. Powers, Lieutenant Colonel, US Army (Ret),
Airborne, Infantry

"This is a well-written book. It tells about a great man dedicated to duty, honor, and sacrifice, both to family and country. You show the great courage he demonstrated in three wars, covering WW2, Korea, and Vietnam. Lieutenant Colonel Gordon Lippman set the example for every other officer to follow by his leadership, courage, bravery, and actions. A must-read for every cadet. KUDOS."

—Darrel Nash, 24th Infantry Regiment Historian

Honor Through Sacrifice:
The Story of One of America's
Greatest Military Leaders

by Robert E. Lofthouse

© Copyright 2021 Robert E. Lofthouse

ISBN 978-1-64663-474-3

Published by

köehlerbooks ™

3705 Shore Drive
Virginia Beach, VA 23455
800-435-4811
www.koehlerbooks.com

HONOR
THROUGH
SACRIFICE

THE STORY OF ONE OF AMERICA'S
GREATEST MILITARY LEADERS

ROBERT E. LOFTHOUSE

VIRGINIA BEACH
CAPE CHARLES

CONTENTS

FOREWORD

YOU ARE ABOUT TO READ the story of a remarkable man and remarkable soldier. Author Robert Lofthouse has the good fortune and privilege of being part of Gordon Lippmann's extended family. But, since Gordon was a lieutenant colonel and I was a captain when we met and served together, he will always be Colonel Lippman to me. You will find that I knew him for just a short time—and that was near the end of his life.

As you read you will quickly realize that Gordon was a warrior in the best sense of the word. So, it would be understandable if he had resented being the executive officer (XO) rather than the commander of an infantry brigade. No one knows what was in his heart, but if he ever felt such resentment, it never showed. Playing the hand he was dealt, he was the best XO a commander could ever hope for. One of his responsibilities as XO was looking after the various supporting units (such as my engineer company) that were not officially a part of the brigade. From our standpoint, as with that of the brigade commander, he was all we could have hoped for.

Our armed services, in training individuals to be officers, teach a lot of things in the category of leadership principles. In my opinion, all of these can be boiled down to two: be smart and be compassionate. Most of us can do those things much of the time, but it is extremely rare to find someone who does both consistently. In a full military career, I was lucky enough to know two officers in this category, and Gordon Lippman was one. To know him, even briefly, was truly an honor.

Jay Franz
Lieutenant Colonel, US Army (Retired)
Tucson, Arizona

INTRODUCTION

THIS IS A STORY ABOUT a man named Gordon Joseph Lippman, a common man displaying uncommon valor. I knew Gordon as my cousin, though not as well as I would have liked. I heard many stories about him when I was younger, and many of those stories continue to be told by his family today.

While researching my family heritage, I wanted to write a biography on one of our family patriots whom I've met and that many family members still remember today. So, I got in touch with the now-adult Lippman children for their recollections and approval to recount this chronicle about their dad.

Gordon and I met in 1965 when I was a teenager and he was getting ready to deploy to Vietnam. I reacquainted myself with him later through our family genealogical research, which my mother handed off to me as the caretaker of our family history. A whole new universe of knowledge and awareness began to emerge for me about many contributions my ancestors made to this great nation from time before its founding.

A hero is a person who is admired or idealized for courage, outstanding achievements, or noble qualities. We need heroes today, and Gordon fits this description. I researched his life growing up in Lemmon, South Dakota, assembled traditional family stories handed down, and incorporated some historical perspective on the events that shaped his life. All of this impacted my perception of him in a positive way.

I wrote this story from a deep belief in, and appreciation for, my biographical subject—motivation which I share with people of faith, scientists, artists, poets, and others who look at their subjects in the same way.

Determined to live my own life vibrantly to the end, as he did, I am telling his story with less interest in the money to be earned than the recounting of this fascinating narrative of leadership, humility, courage, faith, and loyalty.

The rhythm of the story takes us from the present on an illuminating walk through Gordon's life, discovering little known truths about him amid the landscape of the history that he helped to write.

Much of what I've learned about him has been gathered from historical army accounts of the battles he fought, genealogical research, a treasure trove of personal letters to his family, and eye-witness testimonies from those who served with him. I also read a large number of books written about battlefield accounts of his battles in Southern France, Belgium, Korea, and Vietnam showing that his units were in the fight every step of the way. These fights had a specific purpose and people were liberated—that was the just cause he led his men to fight for.

Personal information provided by his loving children also tells the story of a loving father and devoted husband.

From Deacon Robert Hinsdale's unfortunate end in 1675 (memorialized in the Massachusetts State Historical Society as the Battle of Bloody Brook), a long line of his descendants ties in with the storied Remington family lineage. Mary Remington, Frederick Remington's cousin and Deacon Hinsdale's sixth great-granddaughter, married my maternal great-grandfather William Ellis Swan II, from whom Gordon Joseph Lippman and I both descend as first cousins.

The Remington Arms Company was founded in 1840 by our cousin Eliphalet Remington. Famous nineteenth century artist Frederick Remington is our second cousin. Revolutionary War hero Colonel Benjamin Talmadge, Declaration of Independence signer Stephen Hopkins and Vice President Levi P. Morton are all notable cousins of ours, and we are all somehow intertwined in this Hinsdale-Remington-Swan family.

Men and women like Gordon and our ancestors noted above are among those responsible for the freedoms we enjoy today. By contextualizing the history of significant world events and putting this man's place in history into clearer focus, you will learn about one of the most highly decorated members of my family, watching him snatch victory from certain defeat in devoted service to the American ideals of truth, freedom, and justice.

You will be introduced to his character, family, accomplishments, influencers, decisions he made, articles he wrote, and those people who served side by side with him—enduring skirmishes and spending many rain-soaked or freeing cold winter nights in muddy fox holes together. As you read his story, I hope you'll find Gordon Lippman to be an inspiration to you!

It didn't take long for his fellow soldiers to figure out that Gordon Lippman was the man they wanted to follow into battle.

He was one of those studs that came out of small-town America and became a member of *The Greatest Generation*, as Tom Brokaw called them in his book of the same name. He was a young man from the dustbowl, the windswept prairie of South Dakota, growing up during the Great Depression and maturing quickly into a high-impact leader.

Honor Through Sacrifice tells the story about this prairie boy attracting the attention of peers and superiors with his special gifts, skills, and leadership abilities. He overcame great challenges in the army and focused on the mission at hand while enemy bullets whizzed past his head, ricocheted off rocks, and dug into the dirt around his feet.

Repeatedly fighting off fascist and communist aggression, he met and beat the ultimate tests of courage, truth, and honesty under fire. Earning three Purple Hearts, two Bronze Stars, two Silver Stars, a Distinguished Service Cross, Distinguished Service Medal, and numerous other awards from the United States, France, Belgium, South Korea, and South Vietnam along the way, Gordon became one of only 325 infantrymen to earn the Combat Infantry Badge with two stars before the end of the Vietnam War.

Gordon found his vocation in the military after humble beginnings in the Dakotas of the 1930s. He learned his craft well, earning battlefield promotions by doing what was right and what was hard. He led by example, made wise decisions, and taught proper tactics to his troopers.

Although they didn't know Gordon personally, tens of thousands of troopers and citizens from American, Italian, English, French, Belgium, German, Korean, and Vietnamese heritage were grateful that he made that decision. They have had better life opportunities because of how he led and fought for their liberty and freedom. Where does America get such gallant men? He was but one, along with millions of others, who raised his hand to volunteer, and swore a similar oath:

> I, Gordon Joseph Lippman, do solemnly affirm that I will support and defend the Constitution of the United States against all enemies, foreign and domestic; that I will bear true faith and allegiance to the same; and that I will obey the orders of the

president of the United States and the orders of the officers appointed over me, according to regulations and the Uniform Code of Military Justice. So help me God.

Beginning his army career at the age of eighteen, Gordon worked his way into a leadership role at the celebrated Camp Toccoa in northern Georgia. Through cunning, daring, and courageous leadership, he earned the respect of his troopers on and off the battlefield. Eyewitness accounts of his bravery, retraced in story after story, attest to his steadfast leadership and bravery.

He was one of the good patriots. Loving his country, he boldly supported and defended it. His life teaches us much about courage, commitment, and loyalty.

Eating more combat dust than most, he led troops in combat campaigns through Italy, southern France, at the Battle of the Bulge, in the German Hürtgen Forest, and more. In Korea, he led a segregated Black company up and down and back up the Peninsula, pushing the Communist aggressors north of the Thirty-Eighth Parallel.

Later on, as a brigade executive officer in South Vietnam, he led men young enough to be his sons while fighting the Viet Cong (VC) in the Iron Triangle. Through all of this, Gordon maintained his integrity, took care of his men, and did it so that his sons wouldn't have to go to war. As a student of history and international relations, he taught battlefield tactics and believed in the value of fighting to liberate people from their despotic rulers.

It's often said that if we don't study our own history, we will be doomed to repeat it. This is true mainly because we can learn great lessons from it and use them in our own lives to grow. Gordon was a student of history.

His courage to do the right thing inspired the unwavering support of his men, who were dedicated to beating back fanatical enemies. Gordon carried with him a warrior spirit and determination that endeared him to his troopers. As Lyle Rishell wrote in his 1993 book *With a Black Platoon in Combat*, Gordon was "a fine officer, a strong leader, fair minded, and an inspiration to all." That sentiment was echoed by Captain William Hash, Gordon's commanding officer in Korea.

With a sweeping sea-tide kind of change in the political attitudes of five presidential administrations from 1943 through 1965, the national appetite for war diminished in the face of Communist aggression in Southeast Asia. Following the overwhelming Allied victories over the Axis Powers in 1945, America scaled back its military and found itself unprepared to face another global threat when the North Korean Army crossed the Thirty-Eighth Parallel and invaded South Korea.

You will read about how he maintained his objectives while those above him seemed to be losing their political minds. President Truman's post-war decisions about Korea and Vietnam are unfortunately good examples. President Johnson's attitude about Vietnam was another.

While World War II was one of the most cataclysmic conflicts in human history, it was the classic tale of good versus evil: Americans sided with good, and millions across the globe were liberated as a result. Korea and Vietnam have been called controversial at their core, as the United States aimed to eradicate threats to freedom by invading armies from the Soviet Union, North Korea, China, and North Vietnam.

Segregationist attitudes in America surrounded him as he led a maligned Black company into battle. Together, they faced down a formidable North Korean Army and held the line for an uneasy truce that ultimately called a halt to open hostilities in the Korean War.

Fourteen years following his Korean experiences, the political mess resulting in the most disappointing US military defeat in history—capitulation in Vietnam—brings this story to a close.

He brought out the best in people against unconscionable odds, and as a father, he protected, nurtured, and loved his wife and children.

His life is a testimony to standing firm, remaining true to his beliefs, and being steadfastly loyal. If you want to be a great leader who brings out the best qualities in people, one key is to be authentic. Gordon developed quickly into a trustworthy leader. He strove—on and off the battlefield—to keep his focus and faith in Jesus Christ, to hold fast to hard truths, to do the right thing in all the confusion surrounding him, to remain honest, to care for and protect others, and to have the courage to press on no matter what obstacles he faced.

These are the pillars of a good human being that Gordon learned at a young age and refined throughout his life. In the pages that follow, you will read about principles that steered Gordon's mental focus. You will learn more about how he accomplished it all. Those principles necessarily emerged as he matured, but not in a linear fashion. These are significant in and of themselves and together form a comprehensive picture of what drove him to excel at each stage of his life.

In summary, while serving this great nation to combat Nazi fascism and Soviet and Chinese communism, South Dakota native Gordon Lippman helped to free millions of people from an oppressive life by leading his men in more than twenty close-combat battles stretching over eleven military campaigns in a twenty-two-year career. Upon learning of his combat death, his mother remarked that the only thing that got her through the day was knowing that Gordon died while doing what he loved.

The Brigade compound where Gordon served his final days was renamed *Camp Gordon J. Lippman* in his honor.

He was written about in numerous books including *No Place to Die: The Agony of Vietnam* by Hugh Mulligan, and *With a Black Platoon in Combat* by Lyle Rishell. He was interviewed for *Black Soldier White Army: 24th Infantry Regiment in Korea* by William Bowers, William Hammond, and George MacGarrigle.

He was remembered on the 517th PRCT Association website, eulogized on Paul Harvey's radio program on December 30, 1965, included in a 1966 issue of *Readers Digest* and the December 27, 1965 issue of *Newsweek*. His story was recounted on the "Harry Reasoner Report" for *CBS Evening News* on December 28, 1965, and he was honored in *South Dakota Magazine*. A Texas high school produced several individual videos on veterans of the Vietnam War and Gordon was included among them.

Some of the sources referenced within have been lightly edited for clarity, but pulling all of these pieces together in one place, I'm honored to say that his legacy will live on in this manuscript.

Enjoy your nostalgic journey back in time and please honor with me the legacy of this great man. As Paul Harvey said on his radio broadcast eulogizing Gordon on December 30, 1965, "You're about to hear the rest of the story."

CHAPTER 1

GROWING UP IN LEMMON

LITTLE DID ANYONE KNOW THAT at age twenty-seven, he would be making split-second life-or-death decisions while facing North Korean Army machine gunners. Seeing his unit pinned down under withering enemy fire, Gordon rushed the North Korean machine-gun nests to draw their attention while his men advanced. Wounded, and with his ammunition expended, he threw his C rations at the gunners to keep their attention focused on him. His quick thinking preoccupied the shooters long enough to help save his advancing company of soldiers who ultimately won the battle as his men overwhelmed the enemy position. This boy from Lemmon would go on to win the Distinguished Service Cross for his actions and join his fellow South Dakota warriors as a hero among heroes.

HUMILITY

Eugene Swan, his maternal grandfather, showed Gordon that humility did not equate to timidity. He treated this as a virtue. Humility is a wise characteristic that God gave to Gordon—a sense of awe, a sense of wonder, an awareness of the human soul and spirit, and an understanding that there is something unique about every individual, but something bigger than one's self. He grasped the distance between us and the stars, exhibiting a deep faith in God, with an assurance that we're all part of God's great plan in this great universe. Referred to as a *saint* by family members, he maintained and exhibited an endearing modesty about who he was.

GERMAN, SCOTTISH, AND FRENCH-CANADIAN ANCESTRY

Gordon's paternal grandpa, Paul Charles Lippman, emigrated with his brother and sister from Berlin, Germany, in the late nineteenth century to a small German enclave near Minneapolis, Minnesota. Their surname at the time of arrival was Lipnitz.

Assimilating into the American culture was one reason why so many immigrants changed their surnames during that time. While some came with the idea of working for a while and then returning home, most came to stay. Many wanted to become Americans as fast as possible, so they changed their style of clothing and adopted more Americanized names.

Paul and his siblings were teenagers at the time of their arrival and were especially eager to assimilate. With their friends at school urging them to modernize their name, they may not have wanted to be saddled with an old-fashioned European name, so they followed suit with their friends and dropped the German sounding Lipnitz for the English sounding Lippman surname.

Paul attended business school in Minneapolis, where he met his future wife, Edith. They were married at school's end in 1903, and baby boy Harold was born that same year, becoming their only child.

After moving to Lemmon four years later, around when that town was founded in 1907, Paul created a lucrative business opportunity by building the Dakota Implement Company. His was one of the first retail operations in the town where he sold Chevrolets, Buicks, and John Deere equipment. Paved roads were still a thing of the distant future but this cattle town proved to be a rewarding opportunity for the young entrepreneur.

Not wanting to be ostracized as Germans with the outbreak of World War I, Paul maintained his surname as Lippman and worked hard to assimilate into the American culture. He signed his WWI draft card with his English surname and became fluent with his newly adopted language. The war he never entered was fought against his former homeland, a nation's army his grandson would valiantly fight against within a few decades.

Gordon's mother, Arlene, was born into the Swan family in 1903. They were a poor family from Wisconsin Rapids, Wisconsin, descended from Scottish and French-Canadian ancestry. The oldest of five sisters and one brother, Arlene moved with the family to the growing town of Lemmon, South Dakota, where she met Harold, while attending Lemmon parochial and public schools.

Harold and Arleen eventually married at the age of eighteen in 1921. Shortly after, the Swan family—minus Arleen—moved to Zap, North Dakota, where Grandpa Eugene worked as an accountant and foreman in the Lucky Strike Coal Mine.

While visiting her parents in Zap three years later, Arleen gave birth to the third of her five children. Gordon Joseph Lippman came into the world on November 25, 1924. Immediately after his birth, mother and son returned home to Lemmon.

The town of Lemmon was relatively young when Gordon was born. George Ed Lemmon, a long-time cattleman in the area, had settled his ranch near the present site of Lemmon in 1902 and signed a lease covering more than eight hundred thousand acres of land on the Standing Rock Reservation. The town was founded in 1907 as Tent Town, but later renamed in honor of the man who started the settlement.

One-room schoolhouses, wooden walkways, water pumps in the kitchen, and outhouses behind the shed were prevalent, and paved roads did not exist. The railroad kept the cattle commerce flowing in and out of town. It is unfortunate that, in a sign of the times, Black people were not welcome in the town. According to a *Dallas Express* newspaper report on November 29, 1919, two Black men were approached and asked to leave the town and not return. This was the cultural environment in which Gordon was raised, but as we'll see later in his life, it was not the behavior he adopted.

The population of Lemmon had grown to about 1,200 at the time of his birth. As soon as he was of school age, he followed in the footsteps of his older sisters, attending St. Mary's Catholic Grammar School and Lemmon High School.

In 1928, when young Gordon was four years old, Paul and Edith decided to sell their business, retire, and move to the West Coast. They sold Dakota Implement Company and their home, relocating from the bitter cold of the northern plains to the sublime warmth and palm-tree beauty of Los Angeles, California.

Paul died one year later, becoming the victim of a roadside murder during a driving trip back to Lemmon for a debt collection. Edith chose to remain in Los Angeles, sharing a bungalow with her mother, Minnie Prichard. Why am I telling you this? Grandma Edith, never far from the hearts of her grandkids, will come back into this story.

That same year, 1929, the New York Stock Exchange crashed and money started to dry up, causing a rolling wave of extreme financial hardship around the nation. People lost their livelihoods, their homes, and even their families. Some committed suicide because of their hysteria. Times were tough through the next decade, called the Great Depression.

Harold's job at Dakota Implement had produced enough income that he could eventually build his own Lemmon home in 1930. Their youngest child, Paul, was born in 1932. As an adult, he went on to serve time in the US Army as a paratrooper and then became a prolific sportswriter, author of travel books, and editor at the *San Francisco Examiner*.

Due to the sinking economy, deepening recession and drop in sales revenue, Harold lost his job at Dakota Implement. Unable to find other work and sustain a livelihood, he did what other unemployed men in the 1930s did: He joined with the WPA.

President Franklin D. Roosevelt created the Works Progress Administration (WPA) with an executive order on May 6, 1935. It was part of his New Deal plan to lift the country out of the Great Depression caused by the stock market crash. He planned to reform the financial system and restore the economy to pre-Depression levels. The unemployment rate in 1935 was at a staggering 20 percent. The WPA was designed to provide relief for the unemployed by providing jobs and income for millions of Americans.

Harold became one of those WPA workers. He had to put food on the table for his wife and five children, who now ranged in age from three to thirteen. By joining the WPA, Harold, like millions of other men of that era, found steady manual labor and reliable income repairing roads and building fences and bridges. He redeemed himself from the unemployment line.

During the next few years, as weapon production for World War II began ramping up and unemployment dropped, the federal government decided a national relief program was no longer needed, so the WPA was shut down in June 1943. At that time, unemployment in the country was less than 2 percent. Many Americans had transitioned to work in the armed services and defense industries, which is where Harold went next—the Army Munition Depot near Rapid City, South Dakota.

Life in small town South Dakota was simple.

With the severe worldwide economic backdrop of the Depression, at the age of thirteen in 1937, Gordon was able to focus on and achieve a first-class scout rating with the Boy Scouts of America.

Like his mother, Arleen, grandmothers Swan and Lippman before him, Gordon became very active. The ladies had raised large families and were engaged in civic affairs at a time when women's suffrage was gaining momentum. Arleen went on to buy and run a small business, cofound a Toastmistress Club (feminine version of Toastmasters), and cofound a chapter of the Daughters of the American Revolution, collaborating with others in common causes. While in high school, Gordon developed into an enthusiastic student-athlete. He lettered in basketball and football, joined the camera club, and served on the staffs of the theater and yearbook. He was a yell leader and became an honor student. Selected as a member of Lemmon's first Boys State contingent in his junior year, Gordon learned about the rights, privileges, and responsibilities of citizens.

In 1942, Gordon represented Lemmon High School in a district journalistic society capacity as a vice president, elected by delegates of eight schools.

The description of the delegates' duties was spelled out in the school yearbook, *The Lariat*: "Deadlines to meet, assignments to cover, material to be typed, and the everlasting headlines to be written all aided in the nervous system of those who worked. . . Midnight and dawn were among the regular working hours of the conscientious editors, columnists, and the ever-helpful adviser."

A quote from the 1941 *Lariat* shows Gordon to be an accomplished actor as well. "He joined the Thespian Society in his junior year and on November twentieth, the big night for twenty-four new students of the *drahma*, with shaking knees and clammy hands, Gordon made the junior play, *Growing Pains*, the subject of conversation long after the curtain closed. This comedy of youth, puppy love, and parental bewilderment brought forth howls of laughter from even the most hardened critic.

"Gordon, romping through three acts, characterizing a love struck teenster who is also car-crazy, highlighted the play. The luckless parents spent most of their time wondering what would happen next while the neighborhood vamp proceeded to steal the heart of every eligible male in sight, including Gordon. Gordon, rejected by the girl of his dreams, recovered quickly enough to fall in love with a new neighbor whose tactics suspiciously resembled her predecessors."

Ever the adventurous kid and looking for something bigger than Lemmon, Gordon left high school early with parental permission. He boarded a Chicago and Northwestern Railway train in Omaha heading for Los Angeles in the summer of 1942. We don't know what propelled him to leave the plains for Southern California, but the move proved to be transitory.

Once in Los Angeles he moved in with Grandma Edith and her mother. Not long after his arrival, Edith bought eighteen-year-old Gordon an old Model A automobile with a rumble seat. This vehicle was more than ten years old but gave him wheels to seek a job in war-time Los Angeles.

The car was purchased for an economical sixty dollars, a humble beginning indeed. The Model A must have been a sturdy and reliable car, as it carried him all the way back to Lemmon from Los Angeles on narrow and somewhat questionable mid-century roads.

The trip took him more than a week, as the old highways were state and county roads, built prior to the interstate highway system we know today that wouldn't be developed for another fifteen years. Continuing his adventure, he found that roadside hotels and motels were few and very far between. There was no such thing as a fast-food restaurant along the highways in 1943. A short time later, not finding anything to keep him in South Dakota, he returned to Los Angeles to begin working at Smith's Market in Compton.

WAR BONDS

During WWII, the United States government needed to raise money to support the war effort that began in earnest after both Japan and Germany declared war on America.

The first Series E US Savings Bond was sold to President Roosevelt by Treasury Secretary Henry Morgenthau. The bonds sold at 75 percent of their face value in denominations of $25 up to $10,000, with some limitations. In the name of defense of American liberty and democracy, and as safe havens for investment, the public was continually urged to buy bonds.

An emotional appeal went out to citizens by means of advertising. Even though the bonds offered a rate of return below the market value, it represented a moral and financial stake in the war effort. The government recruited New York's best advertising agencies, famous entertainers, and even used familiar comic strip characters to further their appeal. In its advertisements, the New York Stock Exchange urged buyers not to cash in their bonds.

More than a quarter of a billion dollars' worth of advertising was donated during the first three years of the National Defense Savings Program. Massive advertising campaigns used any means of media possible, and the campaign was a huge success. Word spread quickly; polls indicated after only one month that 90 percent of those responding were aware of war bonds. Bonds became the ideal channel for those on the home front to contribute to the national defense.

Bond rallies were held throughout the country with famous celebrities, usually Hollywood film stars, to enhance the advertising's effectiveness. Free movie days were held in theaters nationwide with a bond purchase as the admission. Such popular Hollywood stars as Greer Garson, Bette Davis, and Rita Hayworth completed seven tours in more than three hundred cities and towns to promote war bonds. The Stars Over America bond blitz, in which 337 stars took part, surpassed its quota and netted $838,540,000 worth of bonds.

Rockwell USO cover

Local clubs, organizations, movie theaters and hotels also did their part with their own advertisements. Even the Girl Scouts became involved, with each Scout donating one stamp. Those stamps, starting at ten cents each, were then traded into the national organization for the purchase of war bonds. American artist Norman Rockwell created a series of illustrations in 1941 that became a centerpiece of war bond advertising. *The Saturday Evening Post* reproduced and circulated them, much to the public's approval.

While Rockwell was the most notable artist of war bonds, Irving Berlin was the most celebrated composer. Celebrated for his composition, "God Bless America," he also wrote a song entitled "Any Bonds Today?" and it became the theme song of the Treasury Department's National Defense Savings Program. The famous Andrew Sisters were among the primary performers of this historic song.

One of the most successful single events was a sixteen-hour marathon radio broadcast on CBS, during which nearly forty million dollars' worth of bonds were sold. The marathon featured singer Kate Smith, famous for her rendition of "God Bless America."

Patriotism and the spirit of sacrifice could be expressed with war bond purchases. Millions jumped aboard and billions were raised in the war bond effort.

An unusual baseball game took place in New York City with the New York Yankees, the New York Giants, and the Brooklyn Dodgers. Each of the teams came to bat six times in the same nine-inning game. The attendance plan for the Tri-Cornered Game called for each fan to buy a War Bond as a ticket. There were to be 40,000 unreserved tickets at a cost of $25 each (the bond maturity value), 5,809 reserved seats in the lower stands, each costing a $100 bond, and 3,796 box seats for $1,000 bonds each. That in itself added up to 49,605 fans who pledged $4,416,925. To put this amount in perspective, a $25 War Bond in 1944 actually cost each fan $18.75 (the matured bond could be cashed in for $25); $25 would be worth about $334 in 2014, if multiplied by the annual percentage increases in the Consumer Price Index.

In addition to the amount raised by fans, New York Mayor Fiorello La Guardia announced that the city would purchase $50 million in War Bonds. And the Bond Clothing Stores chain purchased a $1 million bond in exchange for an autographed scorecard of the game. Their final score was the Dodgers 5, Yankees 1, and the Giants 0, *and* the US Government was $56,500,000 richer in war bond sales.

After the end of World War II, January 3, 1946, the last proceeds from the Victory War Bond campaign were deposited into the US Treasury. More than eighty-five million Americans—half the population at that time—purchased bonds, totaling $185.7 billion. Those incredible results, due to the mass selling efforts of helping to finance the war, have never been matched.

A NEW BEGINNING

While Gordon busied himself with his new job, stocking shelves, sweeping floors, and carrying groceries for customers, he became increasingly aware of this war bond effort. Gordon wanted to do his part to help the country.

Seven short months later, he enlisted in the United States Army at the age of eighteen. Joining the Army was potentially a career opportunity and a steady source of income. But mostly, it was the right thing to do for his country.

He signed up to be a paratrooper, enticed by the extra pay and excitement of jumping out of a flying aircraft. After enlisting in March 1943, he shipped out to northern Georgia where he became an elite paratrooper and underwent the strictest form of discipline, something he had not yet seen in his young life.

Gordon spent the next six months in basic training at the Camp Toccoa. Once accepted through the bootcamp screening process, he was assigned to the newly formed 517th Parachute Regimental Combat Team (PRCT).

Gordon Joseph Lippman was on his way to the biggest adventure of his young life.

CHAPTER 2

CAMP TOCCOA

Convinced by 1943 that the assault upon Nazi-held Europe would yield swiftly to elite troops, the US Army created parachute regimental combat teams (PRCT). Drawing on daring volunteers willing to hurl themselves from airplanes and hit the ground fighting, the 517th PRCT became one of the most highly trained airborne units in the world.

—GERALD ASTOR, *BATTLING BUZZARDS: THE ODYSSEY OF THE 517TH PARACHUTE REGIMENTAL COMBAT TEAM 1943-1945*

STRENGTH

Gordon, like his mother Arleen, was strong but not impolite. Taking that extra step to become a powerful, capable leader with a wide reach, he didn't mistake rudeness for strength. Arleen was a sweet woman who could be cuddly and lovable, but she also had a ferocious side when it became necessary to protect her own.

In an age where women were becoming more assertive and engaged in the war effort and business outside the home, she established her own grocery business and helped to start a local Chamber of Commerce as well as a local DAR (Daughters of the American Revolution) chapter. Like his mother, Gordon had the strength of character to take care of his own but kept his focus on what he needed to do in order to survive.

THE RIGHT THING TO DO

All great leaders work on themselves, finding flaws and aspects of their character they want to improve upon and then adjusting their thought processes, behavior, and emotional control. The old adage that practice makes perfect was a seamless constant in Gordon's life.

As Winston Churchill once said to the British people, "Things are not always right because they are hard, but if they are right, one must not mind if they are also hard."

Joining the Allied fight against Nazi fascism was the right thing to do.

Defending freedom-loving people also was the right thing to do.

And while all that is true, Camp Toccoa was hard.

Gordon entered Camp Toccoa as an eighteen-year-old private E-1, one of many. Out of the nine thousand volunteers who tried out, interviewed, and were physically and mentally tested, only twenty-four hundred were accepted. No participation trophies handed out here. Gordon was selected to go through a rigorous physical and mental conditioning process. Private Lippman was quickly recognized for his qualities, his ability to get other troopers to do what was necessary—what was right—to overcome what was hard and to follow orders, all propelling him into a leadership role of his assigned platoon.

Principles taught to him by his parents, grandparents, teachers, coaches, Boy Scouts, and Boys State were impressed upon him throughout his childhood to the point where he deployed them at will, constantly refining his skills.

A few months later, he graduated Toccoa as a staff sergeant E-6, one of the few in charge of a platoon—elite troopers in one of the most highly trained airborne units in the world.

Some perspective is important at this point. Gordon was eighteen years old, had not yet graduated from high school, and was in charge of about thirty-two men who had responsibilities for the heavier crew-served weapons of the battalion. Think about that for a moment the next time an eighteen-year-old boy playing his video game complains about how tough his life has become. These young men found a purpose in their lives and were willing to work hard to develop necessary skills to excel at their craft.

ACTIVATION AND TRAINING

1943   1945

517th shoulder patch

The 517th Parachute Regimental Combat Team was formed from units of the 17th Airborne Division, which was activated on March 15, 1943.

On activation, the regiment had a total strength of nine officers, headed by newly appointed thirty-two-year-old commanding officer Lieutenant Colonel (Lt. Col.) Louis A. Walsh, Jr. Lt. Col. Walsh had been with the airborne since its earliest days and had spent three months as an observer with US forces in the Southwest Pacific. Lt. Col. Walsh was known for setting extremely high standards, including physical conditioning.

Each trooper was required to qualify as *expert* with his individual weapon, *sharpshooter* with another and *marksman* with all crew-served weapons in his platoon.

For the next several months, all men volunteering for parachute duty at induction stations throughout the United States were sent to Camp Toccoa. The division's parachute units were the 517th Parachute Infantry Regiment, the 460th Parachute Field Artillery Battalion and Company C, 139th (C/139) Airborne Engineer Battalion. The 517th trained at Camp Toccoa, Georgia, while the 460th and C/139 trained at Camp Mackall, North Carolina.

Volunteers were screened and trained at Camp Toccoa. The 517th officers were charged with screening the volunteers and assigning those qualified to either infantry, artillery, or engineers. Officers of the 460th and C/139 were placed on temporary duty at Toccoa to help with screening the men. They were joined three days after formation by the cadre under the command of Major William J. Boyle, bringing the regiment's strength in those early days to about 250.

Major Boyle, also known as "Wild Bill" Boyle, was a West Point Class of '39 graduate. His extraordinary courage during WWII would save numerous American lives and earn him the Distinguished Service Cross, the nation's second highest honor for combat service. Nicknamed "Wild Bill" by his men for his strict work ethic and readiness to drop rank with anyone who challenged his leadership, Boyle had little use for spit-and-polish discipline. His drumbeat was all about combat reliability, which he understood was the product of rigorous training and mental toughness. In seven months of war, he had asked nothing of his men that he wasn't prepared to do himself. "Colonel Boyle walked ahead of me a lot of times, and I was the first scout," one soldier remembered. "That was the kind of guy he was. Brave, very brave." Wild Bill became Gordon's battalion commander and his military inspiration.

The Army eventually interviewed more than three thousand men to get eight hundred for each battalion. With three battalions in the regiment, about 2,400 men would have to be trained, equipped, and prepared for war. Not just anyone made the grade, but once a recruit was accepted, the 517th gave them their basic training.

Two days before the cadre's arrival, the first trainload of volunteers pulled into the railroad station at Toccoa, early and unexpected. Nine officers met the train, drove the recruits to camp in borrowed trucks, issued some military clothing and bedding and—with some help from the post garrison—cooked and served them their first meal.

They were the first of many. *The Paratroopers' Odyssey*, a book compiled in 1985 by Clark Archer, tells the historical story of the 517th Parachute Infantry Regiment. This is the official history of the unit, taken directly from the morning reports and other military records, as well as firsthand accounts of the troopers, and reveals for us what daily life was like in that boot camp. Here is an excerpt:

Through the spring of 1943, trains arrived at Toccoa daily with contingents of fifty to 150 men. Each group was met at the station and trucked to the parade ground, where a thirty-four-foot-tall parachute *mock tower* had been erected.

Lieutenant John Alicki, a veteran of the Japanese surprise raid on Pearl Harbor, favored by fortune with a rugged appearance, greeted them with a blood-and-guts speech intended to scare off the timorous.

"Awright, ya volunteered for parachute duty, now's your chance to prove you meant it!" *Boom Boom,* Alicki would bark. Still in civilian clothing, each man climbed the tower, strapped into a parachute harness for the first time in their lives, was tapped on the rump, and jumped. Most made it. Those who did not were immediately headed elsewhere.

Receiving and screening one to two hundred men a day was a pretty big order for the 517th.

In and out platoons were formed. Those who survived the mock tower went to the *in* platoon for further screening. This consisted of a medical examination by Regimental Surgeon Paul Vella and his staff, followed by an interrogation by their potential officers as to why they had applied for parachute duty.

Many answers were interesting, while some were downright hilarious. A few had been advised by doctors to take up parachuting to help overcome their fear of heights. Some with criminal records had been told their slates would be wiped clean if they joined. Those failing the screening process were sent to the *out* platoon and reassigned elsewhere.

On weeknights, school was conducted for about three hours after the evening meal, to get the officers up to speed on Army protocol, infantry tactics, paratrooper tactics, weapons and other areas of great importance to an infantry officer. Classes were held in various subjects ranging from the platoon in the attack to rigging bundles for parachute drops. Field grade officers and senior captains were the instructors.

The Paratroopers Odyssey goes on to say, "After class, the officers were free for what remained of the evening but still had to instruct the troops the next day. Most platoon leaders, almost as inexperienced as the troops they were instructing, managed to stay ahead only by cramming on field manuals long into the night. Despite this harsh regimen—or perhaps because of it—most of the officers and men of the 517th were solidly behind Colonel Walsh. They were proud of themselves and the outfit they represented and ready to follow wherever he might lead."

This is where Gordon learned his basic Army drill, protocol, weapons, jump, and survival skills.

From the incoming manpower, a three-battalion regiment of 142 officers, two warrant officers, and 1,856 enlisted men was created. The Tables of Organization and Equipment for parachute units were restricted by the technology of the time.

Everything had to be deliverable by the parachutes and aircraft available. It was visualized that paratroopers would land on or near their objectives and fight for only a few days before being relieved. Units were to be *lean and mean* with no non-fighters or administrative frills.

The rifle squads were the cutting edge of the sword. There were two per platoon, six per company, and eighteen in each battalion. Each rifle squad consisted of a squad leader, an assistant, a three-man machine gun team, and seven riflemen.

Two such squads and a 60mm mortar squad made a rifle platoon commanded by a lieutenant with an assistant platoon leader, a platoon sergeant, and a few runners. From company through regiment the organization was triangular. Three rifle platoons made a company, three companies a battalion, and three battalions a regiment.

Additional support was provided at battalion and regimental levels. The battalion headquarters company included 81mm mortar and machine gun platoons. At regiment there were headquarters and service companies.

He was an expert shot with rifle and carbine—a level which one qualifies is dependent on the weapon, firing range, and the course of fire. For example, to earn an Army Marksmanship Qualification Badge he must have shot with 90 percent accuracy for expert. Gordon qualified with crew-served machine gun and grenade launcher.

Into this order of structure and discipline, the now nineteen-year-old Gordon entered the European Theater of Operations as a staff sergeant, becoming responsible for leading one of these light machine gun platoons. His career was born in the First Battalion HQ Company. He had earned this leadership position through the toughness that was known as *Currahee*, leading and encouraging his fellow troopers through physical fitness training where they learned the tools and techniques that would serve them well in the upcoming fields of battle.

In order to free company and battalion commanders from administrative chores, the service company was made up of personnel, food service, and supply units. This looked good on paper but did not work out well in practice because the commanders lost control of factors that affected morale. In the 517th, supply sergeants were released to companies and clerks found their way into orderly rooms, but service company operated battalion messes throughout the war.

Anyone who has tried to feed six hundred people at one sitting can imagine the result. Out of necessity the troopers normally subsisted on the individual C and K rations in the field. These were intended only for emergencies, but became the steady diet.

As a fresh recruit Gordon was introduced to rigorous physical training that involved running many miles each day, physical exercise, weapons training, and jumping off a thirty-four-foot tower, learning how to hit the ground with a thud and exercise the agility to keep from breaking his ankles.

Colonel Walsh set extremely high standards. Physical conditioning was paramount. The paratroopers invented jogging thirty years before it became popular. Each morning after reveille the order was bellowed out:

"Riiiight face, double time, maaarch."

The entire command, colonel to private, was off on a two-mile run around camp, in step and in formation. In the afternoon there was either a routine run of six to eight miles or a seven-mile special run up and down Mount Currahee.

Once or twice a week speed marches of five miles in forty minutes were made, with full packs and all weapons—including mortars and machine guns. Throughout all training, pushups were administered as mild punishments.

Working through their development as soldiers and as a unit, the regiment was moved to Fort Benning, Georgia, for parachute training. The 517th completed jump school with no washouts, setting a record that has endured. They were also the first paratroopers to wear steel helmets in jump training, as a modified football helmet had been used up to that time.

On completion of jump training, the first and second battalions moved on to Camp Mackall, while the third remained at Fort Benning to fill up completely. On return to Camp Mackall, Lt. Col. Walsh was replaced as commanding officer by Lt. Col. Rupert D. Graves, United

States Military Academy '24, who came from command of the 551st Parachute Infantry Battalion.

The battalions were filled in numerical sequence. Under Major Boyle, 1st Battalion was filled in April 1943, and 2nd Battalion, under Major Richard J. Seitz, was nearly filled in May. By early July, while Major Melvin Zais' 3rd Battalion was still awaiting its first recruit, the flow of volunteers to Toccoa was suddenly turned off. The third battalion would be completed with parachute school graduates who had already completed basic training.

In February 1944, the regiment moved to Tennessee to take part in maneuvers being conducted by Headquarters US Second Army. In March, it was announced that the parachute elements of the 17th Airborne Division—the 517th Parachute Infantry Regiment (PIR), the 460th Parachute Field Artillery Battalion, and Company C of the 596th Airborne (Parachute) Engineer Company—were being pulled out for overseas shipment as the 517th Regimental Combat Team (RCT).

Now expanded with the additional units and elevated to become a combat team, the 517th RCT was expected to operate as a small division.

In early May, as preparations were made for the 517th RCT to ship overseas, the regiment companies were staged through Camp Patrick Henry near Newport News, Virginia. On May 17, 1944, the 517th boarded the former Grace ocean liner *Santa Rosa*, while the 460th and 596th loaded onto the Panama Canal ship *Cristobal*, destination Italy, although the troopers did not know that yet.

Santa Rosa

Santa Rosa had been requisitioned by the US War Shipping Administration on January 3, 1942 with Grace Line operating the ship as agents while the ship was allocated to the Army for troop service. Even in wartime gray, the ship retained her elegant ocean liner lines.

Santa Rosa was painted in wartime gray like most naval ships of the day, but she still displayed her original beauty—striking twin funnels, sweeping bow, and the long, beautiful lines of a luxury passenger cruise ship. Tied up to the pier, this ship sat motionless in the water, but projected a sensation of speed, luxury, and moonlit tropical nights.

Santa Rosa eventually made twenty-one voyages from the East Coast of the US from 1942–1945; sixteen were to Europe, one to Australia, one to India, and three to Africa. On this voyage, she would transport the 517th RCT to Italy.

While delivering a keynote speech at the 1989 reunion of the 517th Parachute Regimental Combat Team in Nashville, Tennessee, Bill Breuer said, "Those of us who went through it know that war is horrible. But I would do it all again. Sometimes a man has to stand up and fight for what he thinks is right! Where does America get such gallant men?" He went on to quote paratrooper Rudy Hernandez, a Korean War Medal of Honor awardee who suffered disabling wounds. Rudy was asked, "If you could be granted one wish, what would it be?" Rudy pondered the question, then replied softly: "I would like to have the chance to serve my country again." "Where does America get such gallant men," Breuer asked the audience.

CURRAHEE

Currahee Mountain

It seemed fitting that Currahee was the name of the mountain at Camp Toccoa, as it is a Cherokee word that means *stands alone*. It is significant in that paratroopers do stand alone as they drop behind enemy lines. *Currahee* is the battle cry of the 506th Infantry Regiment, which was memorialized in Steven Ambrose's book *Band of Brothers*, and in Steven Spielberg's and Tom Hanks' HBO miniseries of the same name.

Camp Toccoa subjected these young men to many rigorous physical challenges to help prepare them for battle. One notable event was a 115-mile march by members of the 501st Parachute Infantry Regiment from Camp Toccoa to Atlanta over the first three days of December 1942. The three-day hike was a challenge to beat the Japanese record of a similar maneuver.

The roads up Currahee Mountain remain as US Forest Service roads today as a reminder of the quote from training soldiers: "Three miles up. Three miles down," as they used these roads for their hikes and runs.

Including the famed "Band of Brothers" of Easy Company 506th PIR, the following four airborne regiments trained at Toccoa between 1942 and 1943:

506 PIR—101st Airborne Division
>   (Often called the *Five-Oh-Sink*, in honor of their Commander Col. Robert Sink)
>   Camp Toccoa from July 20 to November 15, 1942
>   Campaigns: European—Overlord, Market Garden, Battle of the Bulge
>   Easy Company—Second Battalion
>>   Featured in *Band of Brothers*, written by historian and biographer Stephen E. Ambrose and a ten-part, eleven-hour television World War II miniseries, originally produced and broadcast in 2001. It was directed by Stephen Spielberg and Tom Hanks.

501 PIR—101st Airborne Division
>   Camp Toccoa from November 15, 1942 to March 15, 1943
>   Campaigns: European—Overlord, Market Garden, Battle of the Bulge.

511 PIR—11th Airborne Division
Camp Toccoa from January 5 to March 23, 1943
Campaigns: Philippines—Leyte, Luzon. Participated with
Filipino Guerrillas in liberation of notorious Los Banos
Japanese Prison, often referred to as *Angels at Dawn.*

517 PIRCT—Part of the First Airborne Task Force, then in
intervals with the 17th,
the 82nd and the 13th Airborne Divisions.
Camp Toccoa from March 15 to August 8, 1943
Campaigns: European—Italy, Anzio, France, Dragoon,
Belgium, Battle of the Bulge

*Enlistment motivation occurs once the war or conflict has started,
but the soldier has not yet entered into combat. The army may
have already fought battles, but the individual has not yet taken
part and experienced them. In fact, he may not yet even be a
soldier. The final element of enlistment motivation manifests itself
in an eagerness to enter battle, to observe and take part in the fight.*

**—CAPTAIN TANIA M. CHACO, US ARMY, *WHY DID THEY FIGHT?
AMERICAN AIRBORNE UNITS IN WORLD WAR II***

BECOMING A MAN

Gordon was a young platoon sergeant, about to lead thirty-two
young men onto the field of battle against seasoned Nazi combat
veterans in 1944–45. He hadn't yet graduated from high school, but his
wits, courage, athleticism, and guidance on the training field earned the
respect of his troopers and the recognition of his battalion leadership.

Paratroopers came from all social and economic levels. Most were
teenage kids, but some were married men in their twenties. There

were roughnecks and brawlers, but also some saints and scholars. The common denominators uniting them were a willingness to take a chance and a refusal to admit there was anything in the world they couldn't handle.

Over the course of their brief time together, the 517th Parachute Regimental Combat Team would accumulate more than 150 combat days from August 1944 through June 1945, while engaging in five major campaigns on battlefields in Italy, France, Belgium, and Germany.

The battalion casualty rate was a staggering 81.9 percent. Four out of five would become wounded, killed-in-action or missing. The team suffered 1,576 casualties and 252 men killed-in-action. The fights would be brutal and these men's lives would be forever indelibly marked.

In addition to one Medal of Honor winner, troopers of the 517th PRCT earned 1,576 Purple Hearts, 131 Silver Stars, 631 Bronze Stars, six Distinguished Service Crosses, five Legion of Merits, four Soldier's Medals, two Air Medals, and seventeen French Croix de Guerre's.

Indeed, *where does America get such gallant men?*

Years after WWII, the alumni group of the 517th, the 517 PRCT Association, held annual reunions, printed a quarterly newsletter, and maintained an almost daily email news list so that their accomplishments could be shared, and these men who had endured so much together could remain in contact with one another well into their retirement years. There was also an auxiliary group, consisting of children, relatives, and friends of the 517th who actively assisted in the events and maintained the history of the unit until well into the twenty-first century, a full sixty-five years after the unit was dissolved in 1945.

For additional information and details about the 517th PRCT, go to http://517prct.org.

CHAPTER 3

EUROPEAN WAR

CONFIDENCE

Gordon was proud but not arrogant. He took care in building on his aspirations, not wanting to allow his ego to undermine the team's mission. He was instrumental in helping his men succeed. He cherished the cause of freedom and directed his men along the way to accomplish the goals set out for his team. His key to becoming a good leader was to be confident without being big-headed. He chose to do the right thing and, like Harold during the Depression, he also chose to do the hard thing.

George Rumsey, one of his platoon members from Camp Toccoa and a machine gunner who jumped in France with Gordon, remembers him as a big man, a smart man, a nice guy, and a good leader. "We were trained to be the best of the best, a real band of brothers, just doing our duty," Rumsey said.

HISTORY 1940–1944

The Allies were on the offensive in 1944 after losing the Battle of France on the Western Front and abandoning Europe from May through June 1940.

What happened between 1940 and 1944? For insight on how the Allies turned the tide of the war in Hitler's Fortress Europe, you have to look at the major events and circumstances of the war on the ground before Gordon arrived on the European Continent. While he played no part in combat until late 1944, he was fully engaged in the toughest ground offensive of German Armies during the liberation of Europe.

First, I want to deliberate on his trans-Atlantic boat ride, his journey into combat, and his involvement in Operation Dragoon.

We also need to review some background on why the feared German Army was reeling back on their heels after the Americans entered this war of aggression brought on by Adolf Hitler and the German Third Reich.

1942—THE WEHRMACHT

The *Wehrmacht* formed the heart of Germany's politico-military power. Recounted from *Hitler's Wehrmacht*, by University Press of Kentucky, in the early part of the Second World War, the Wehrmacht employed combined arms tactics (close-cover air support, tanks, and infantry) to devastating effect in what became known as *blitzkrieg* (lightning war). Its campaigns in Poland (1939), France (1940), the Soviet Union (1941), and North Africa (1941–42) are regarded as brilliant acts of boldness that stunned and shocked the people they invaded.

These far-flung advances strained the Wehrmacht's capacity to the breaking point, which culminated in their first major defeat in the Battle of Moscow (1941).

By late 1942, Germany was losing the initiative in all theatres. Their operational art was no match for the war-making abilities of the Allied coalition—now joined by the Americans following Pearl Harbor—which helped to expose the Wehrmacht's weaknesses in strategy, doctrine, and logistics.

With the absence of combat operations on American soil, the

United States was free to gear up manufacturing, logistical distribution, and training unencumbered by enemy attacks. This mass production and nationwide mobilization were a force unmatched by the Axis Powers.

The turning point of World War II was in 1942, and is one of those facts upon which most everyone can agree. This global conflict, more than any other before it, was a vast and sprawling set of interlocking military campaigns on land, sea, and air. It involved hundreds of millions of human beings, from the freezing cold of the Arctic to the sweltering heat of the Burmese jungle, and the notion that there was a single discrete moment that turned it is problematic, to say the least.

Still, it is clear that something important happened in 1942. It was, after all, the year of El Alamein in the African theater, the siege of Leningrad, the battle of Stalingrad, and Operation Barbarossa— all spectacular losses for the Wehrmacht.

But for 1942 to live up to its billing as the "hinge of fate," as Winston Churchill memorably called it, a fatal blow had to be dealt to the German armed forces. Could the Allies, even with their sheer superiority in material and men, pull it off?

In 1942, the German Army turned one last time to its traditional Prussian tactics of maneuver. The Wehrmacht stalled in Russia but continued fighting on two fronts for three more years.

Germany also had been locked in a conflict with Great Britain since September 1939, one that it tried half-heartedly to end in the summer and fall of 1940. But that ended badly in the Battle of Britain where the British Royal Air Force (RAF) repulsed the German *Luftwaffe's* (Air Force) attempt to bomb England into submission.

Beginning in mid-1941, Germany had done nothing but add enemies, declaring war on the United States shortly after Japan bombed Pearl Harbor in Hawaii. The USA became the deadliest and most adept foe the Wehrmacht had faced thus far. German U-boats continued to probe the American East Coast and sink American ships on the high seas. But America was ready for this confrontation.

Germany's next and what was to be its last, major campaign in 1942—the drive to capture the oil fields of the Soviet Caucasus—seemed to offer another textbook opportunity for the Germans to demonstrate sound maneuvering tactics and strategies grounded in more than a century of war-making experience. Including the modern mechanized variant with tanks, blitzkrieg could best the massive forces arrayed against them.

Until the war's end, on the Eastern Front and elsewhere, Germany sought to land a resounding blow against one of its enemies, one hard enough to shatter the enemy coalition, or at least to demonstrate the high price that the Allies would have to pay for victory.

That strategy certainly caused tremendous damage in those last four years, and many historians downplay how alarmingly close Germany came to succeeding.

While Germany's strategy for winning the war in 1942 failed, it did so spectacularly. Was it a war-winning gambit? Was it the best strategy under the circumstances? The German High Command, consisting mostly of the generals, disagreed on strategies. So, this answer depends on your point of view.

It absolutely was an operational posture in complete harmony with German military history and tradition as it unfolded over the centuries. Germany, blinded by its past successes, failed to recognize that they needed to adjust to the coming Allied storm: American immersion in the Allied war effort.

In their push to conquer Europe in the late 1930s, Germany successfully overran their enemies using the blitzkrieg. Russia put an end to that in 1942. The Wehrmacht, following their Prussian war-mongering tactics, provided a classic answer to the question, "What do you do when the blitzkrieg fails?"

You launch another—indeed, a whole series of them.

The centerpiece of 1942 would be another grand offensive in the east. *Unternehmen Blau* (Operation Blue) objectives would include a lunge over the mighty Don River to the Volga, the seizure of the great industrial city of Stalingrad, and finally, a wheel south into the Caucasus, home to some of the world's richest oil fields of that day.

With the final Operation Blue objectives more than a thousand miles from their starting line, no one can accuse Hitler and the high command of thinking small.

But for 1942 to become the *"hinge of fate"*, a fatal blow had to be dealt to the German armed forces. What would the Allies need to do to succeed at grabbing the advantage, and turn the tide of the war?

As previously mentioned, the Soviet Union defeated the Wehrmacht in Moscow—yet one more formidable European army defeated during a bitter Russian winter—first the 19th Century French under Napoleon, and now the 20th Century Germans under Hitler. After having suffered a defeat in Moscow earlier in the year, Hitler turned his forces on Stalingrad for two reasons: it was an industrial hub with access to the Volga River (an important Soviet supply route) and for propagandistic purposes due to the fact the city was named after the Soviet Union's leader, Joseph Stalin.

The German siege of Stalingrad lasted for 263 days through the fall and winter of 1943–44. The Wehrmacht and the Red Army (the Soviet Union's Army) engaged in door-to-door and hand-to-hand combat. But Russian perseverance, numbers, and mostly weather won the struggle.

The Second Battle of El Alamein was the pinnacle of the North African campaign. In October 1942, German and Italian forces met the British infantry on the battlefield but were quickly overwhelmed and forced to retreat to Tunisia. That defeat effectively cut the Wehrmacht off from the Suez Canal and access to the oil fields in the Middle East.

They needed fuel in order to maintain their industrial war machine.

Less than one year later, and in response to the humiliating defeat at Stalingrad, Hitler launched Operation Citadel, a campaign intended to annihilate the Soviet forces around the city of Kursk and to reclaim German dominance in the east.

Allied codebreakers got a hint of this plan and had time to fortify the area with ditches and minefields. Both sides suffered hundreds of thousands of losses, but the Soviet Union eventually was able to drive the Nazis back. The Battle of Kursk was Germany's final offensive attack on the Eastern Front. It is also considered the greatest tank battle of World War II.

To paraphrase Churchill, before 1942 the Allies never won a substantial victory, and after 1942 they never suffered a significant defeat. The tables had turned on the lionized Wehrmacht in the Eastern Front and in Northern Africa. With army forces arrayed on the French Atlantic and Mediterranean coastlines, and both Italian and German armies holding Italy, the German High Command knew an invasion was imminent.

TYPICAL DAY ONBOARD A TROOP SHIP

Gordon and the rest of the 517th was on the way to confront the Wehrmacht. Trans-Atlantic Ocean travel aboard ship was an experience Gordon was not familiar with, and more than a few troopers got ill from the constant rolling motion of the waves, side to side, up and down. But that wasn't the worst of it.

Since the convoy was traveling through the Nazi U-boat submarine net, the ships' companies would constantly put the troopers through readiness drills. A clanging bell would sound, then a slight pause and then the bell would sound again like someone banging on a metal trash can!

The sudden noise unmistakably woke everyone up, with the signal to abandon ship! What a way to start the day, by jumping into the ice-cold water at five in the morning. Maybe around noon the water would be inviting, but at this hour? It was a good way to catch hypothermia.

When the ship was two days passage west of the Strait of Gibraltar, it was well within the snare of the U-boat wolfpack. As the clanging commenced once again—*clang! clang! clang!*—the notion that it was a drill quickly faded.

Gordon's feelings of self-preservation suddenly overwhelmed him, so he quickly pulled on his boots, put on his coat, and grabbed the pillow that doubled as a life jacket. The ladder that led to the deck, as well as the limited open area, was jammed with a frantic mass of humanity.

Being a sound sleeper and a slow riser was definitely a disadvantage during this time of chaos. Discerning the gravity of the situation, a sudden sense of fear settled in.

A voice on the loudspeaker interrupted the clanging to apologize that the wrong signal was given. The convoy was actually under attack by enemy aircraft and all troops were ordered to remain below deck.

In one direction there was a mass of frantic humanity blocking the only authorized way out. The other direction offered a simple escape to the open deck. But the mass of soldiers turned around and scrambled to get back down below. Staying below deck during an attack created a claustrophobic sensation, and sensing a potential catastrophe, the folly of following the crowd became very real.

With the ensuing chaos, noise, and push and pull of people, it soon became clear that if the ship was sunk, escaping into the water may not have been possible. Looking out a cabin portal, Gordon could see hundreds of tracer rounds arcing skyward illuminating the darkness. Standing in awe, fascinated as clusters of fiery trajectories exploded from every ship in the convoy, he witnessed the cruiser escorts' batteries rattling a rhythmic crescendo of anti-aircraft weapons along with the thundering sounds of the cruiser's big guns.

The sights and sounds were fantastic, the most spectacular fireworks display this young teenager ever witnessed—of course until the next time it happened. When the batteries stopped firing, the exhibition faded away. All was dark and very quiet, but only momentarily, as the batteries came to life again spewing tracers upward to invisible targets.

Fire trails arced up and away then faded from sight. Slowly the trajectories swung upward overhead. The attack planes were passing over from side to side but they were too high or it was too dark for the planes to be seen.

After a short delay, the performance was repeated once again. In time, the batteries became silent. The air raid was over and the convoy continued eastward toward Italy.

When the all clear was sounded, a voice came over the speakers again: "The ship suffered no damage and will continue on with the convoy." Some scuttlebutt indicated that several ships got hit, maybe even sunk and hopefully those sailors and troops would be rescued, but the convoy had to keep moving.

A SENSE OF NORMALCY AMID TURMOIL

Shipboard activities included card games, some gambling, weapons training, and calisthenics to keep the men sharp and focused as much as possible on the upcoming mission. Together at Currahee learning how to become soldiers, and now a lot closer together on the *Santa Rosa* dodging submarines, the men coped with boredom the best they could.

Being aboard ship for about two weeks, the troopers enjoyed pleasant weather and calm seas for the most part. Other than the occasional sea hunt by the U-boats, the view rarely varied. In every direction the seascape was monotonously the same, day after day, nothing but water and boats, and rolling seas. The sky above, the sea below and off in the distance on the horizon, the sea and sky met like a great circle around the ship.

An occasional North Atlantic storm whipped up the seas and the ship rocked more violently, leading to even more sick passengers. Several days after the last air raid, this panorama changed abruptly as a mountain began to rise out of the sea. That mountain was Gibraltar, the gateway to the Mediterranean Sea.

One dark night the ships slipped through the Strait of Gibraltar and it soon became obvious that the destination was Italy. After hugging the coast of north Africa for a few days, the transports headed northeast. Off Sardinia there was a little excitement aboard *Santa Rosa* when it came near a floating mine.

A crew member got his rifle and prepared to fire but was called off because the mine was only a few yards from the ship's side. While the spectators held their collective breath waiting for an explosion, the ship sailed on, leaving the mine bobbing wickedly in its wake.

One morning after passing through the Strait of Gibraltar, looking off the bow on the horizon, a triangular peak began jutting up out of the water. As the day wore on, the peak gradually increased in height as if it were rising out of the water. The peak grew in height, showing a widened base and a white top. It looked like a snowcapped mountain.

 As the ship got closer, foothills and land mass came into view and the white-capped peak was indeed a very high mountain. It appeared this illusion might be caused by the curvature of the Earth but that's the impression you get at sea. That peak was Mount Etna, the highest active volcano in all of Europe at 10,800 feet high. As Santa Rosa sailed between Sicily and Sardinia, the Italian mainland soon came sharply into view.

CHAPTER 4

FIRST COMBAT ACTIONS

Courage is fear holding on a minute longer.

—GENERAL GEORGE S. PATTON

MAY 31, 1944—517TH PARACHUTE
INFANTRY COMBAT TEAM LANDS IN ITALY

While the Allies continued making inroads on multiple fronts against the Germans in eastern Europe and north Africa, the *Santa Rosa* docked at Naples, Italy, on May 31 with highly trained recruits who had yet to see war up close. They were led by a cadre of seasoned soldiers. Naples was now under Allied control and was used as a disembarkation point for arriving troops and equipment.

Troopers filed down gangplanks into waiting railroad cars and were carried to a staging area in the Neapolitan suburb of Bagnoli. En route, Colonel Graves was handed an order directing the regiment to take part in the attack from Valmontone to Rome the next day.

The 517th was ready to go, but only with rifles. Since crew-served weapons, artillery, and vehicles had been loaded separately, the regiment would not have its full complement of weapons and equipment off-loaded from the ship for another couple of days. After this was pointed out, the order was cancelled and the regiment moved on to set up camp in the crater bed of a long-extinct volcano, Agnano.

The crater is situated in the Campi Flegrei volcanic region just west of Naples. It is about four miles in circumference and was celebrated by the ancient Greeks and Romans for its hot springs. The six-story *Termae Anianae* (thermal baths) was built for visitors by the Romans.

The men took some time to get accustomed to Italy, secure their gear, and prepare for the coming battle. This was a time of great anxiety and anticipation, and relief for some that the long stormy North Atlantic boat ride from America's East Coast was over. They were on European soil now, getting ready to meet the formidable German Wehrmacht, which was focused on the imminent invasion of the French coast facing Britain and had just lost a major battle at Anzio.

NORMANDY

The Battle of Normandy in France was gearing up to kick off in just seven days—and it lasted from June through August 1944. That invasion resulted in the Allied liberation of western Europe from Nazi Germany's control. Codenamed *Operation Overlord*, the battle began on June 6, 1944 (D-Day), when approximately 156,000 American, British, and Canadian forces landed on five beaches along a fifty-mile stretch of the heavily fortified coastline in the Normandy region of France.

This invasion was the largest amphibious military assault in history and required extensive planning. Prior to D-Day, the Allies conducted a large-scale deception campaign designed to mislead the Germans about the intended invasion target. Following D-Day and by late August 1944, all of northern France had been liberated. There was no turning back, even with the heavy military and civilian casualties, as well as substantial asset and equipment loss.

Allied Command set its sights squarely on Berlin. The Normandy landings have been called the "beginning of the end" of the war in Europe. But, due to a determined and resilient German Wehrmacht resistance, it would take the Allies another year of heartache, botched plans, coordinated battlefield victories and an intense bombing campaign to bring the war to a close.

Eyeball to eyeball, toe to toe with simultaneous battles raging on the Eastern Front and the Western Front, the Allies tightened their grip on the once-formidable Wehrmacht. Germany was in the defensive fight for its very existence.

FIRST DAY OF COMBAT FOR THE 517TH

A week after the troopers landed in Italy, weapons and vehicles gradually began to arrive for the 517th. On June 14, the outfit struck tents, stowed away extra gear, and moved to a Neapolitan beach to wait for the LST (Landing Ship, Tank) ride to Anzio, which was itself just recently liberated following a hard-fought six-month battle.

After another day at sea, the convoy stopped off the coast of Anzio. Staff, regimental, and battalion commanders went ashore to get briefed on the enemy situation and were informed that the destination was Civitavecchia, a coastal town northwest of Rome built in the second century. The Port of Civitavecchia retained some of its original features, like the Roman dock, and contained a sixteenth-century Michelangelo-designed fort.

The convoy resumed sailing through another night at sea, then went ashore on the beach unopposed. The 517th PRCT was then reassigned to Major General Fred L. Walker's 36th Infantry Division, which was operating on the left of the US Fifth Army.

A long truck ride and a short foot march on June 17 brought the units south of Grosseto, where Colonel Graves was handed an overlay marked with zones, objectives, and phase lines. The regiment was directed to join the division's advance north from Grosseto the next day. With all of the preparation, training, boat rides, shipboard boredom, delays, and anticipation, the men of the 517th were ready to get in the fight.

German Field Marshal Albert Kesselring's forces were already in full retreat. An Allied offensive that began in April to draw Wehrmacht troops away from Normandy had finally taken Cassino. Allied forces advancing from the south had linked up with those at Anzio and captured Rome. The German Wehrmacht had been decisively defeated and was moving to a new line above the Arno River on its way out of Italy.

The Italian terrain was ideal for the German defense. The Appenine Mountains run down the spine of the Italian peninsula. Numerous spurs extending east and west formed cross-compartments over which the Allies had to advance. Any hilltop provided good observation and fields of fire. Villages dating from medieval times were perched on hills, and very little effort was required to convert them into fortresses.

The 36th Division was sometimes called *The Texas Army*, because it had been formed around National Guard units from that state. Since landing at Salerno in September of 1943, the division had developed a highly professional attitude toward the war. There was no rush. The Germans had been here yesterday, were here today, and would still be here tomorrow. In contrast, the 517th was green, eager, and anxious to prove itself.

June 18 witnessed the PRCT's first day of combat and the regiment fought like professional soldiers, suffering about fifty casualties but inflicting several times that number on the enemy. The next seven days were spent in almost continuous movement and conflict.

The Wehrmacht tried to make an orderly withdrawal, but the Americans pressed them hard. For the 460th Parachute Field Artillery Battalion, this period involved a continuous twenty-four-hour-a-day operation. Gun batteries continually leapfrogged each other, usually with two batteries remaining in position and firing, while the other two were advancing to help push the line forward.

The principal chore of the 596th Engineers was road reconnaissance and mine-sweeping, clearing a path so the regiment could freely advance on their objectives.

The 517th Second Battalion captured the hilltop village of Montesario on June 19. The Third Battalion moved out on the left through Montepescali against light resistance, taking Sticciano with fourteen prisoners. Meanwhile, the First Battalion had taken Monte Peloso.

The 517th bivouacked overnight on June 22–23 on a ridgeline south of Gavorrano. The next morning, they moved across the Piombino Valley and closed into all assembly areas behind the 142nd Infantry Regiment. On June 24, the Second Battalion entered the eastern outskirts of Follonica under heavy artillery and *Nebelwerfer* (smoke mortar) fire by the enemy.

Later in June, the 517th was taken off the line, getting some much-needed rest and joining IV Corps reserve. They remained there until early July.

Treated to USO shows, PX rations, Coca Cola, cold beer, baseball, boxing, and a tour of the Vatican in Rome, it seemed like a real Roman holiday. When the Vatican heard that American parachutists were camped near Rome, the Pope invited the troopers for an audience.

Troopers also visited some of the famous sites in Rome: Michelangelo's Sistine Chapel, Corso Umberto, the Coliseum, Roman Forum, Victor Emmanuole Monument, the Pantheon, Arch of Constantine, the Appian Way, and took in the ancient Roman aqueducts and catacombs. What a welcome respite from war!

While resting in camp, Corporal Charles E. Pugh of the 596th Parachute Engineer Company, tuned in to Radio Berlin on a hot and humid afternoon. *Axis Sally* was playing a record of "Sentimental Journey," a popular American ballad of the time. After the song concluded, sexy-voiced Axis Sally came on the air. "Hey, all you good-looking guys in the Five Hundred Seventeenth Parachute Regiment outside Rome," she cooed, "you won't have to paint your face black like you did yesterday when you come to southern France."

Sally giggled, then added, "Because we're going to light up the sky so brightly with our *ack-ack* guns that the black faces won't help hide you!"

Several others joined Charlie in the tent and were startled to find out that Sally not only had pinpointed their location but also was aware of the locale where the men would land in France. Now the female propagandist turned bitter and said with a snarl, "Our boys in southern France know how to take care of you vicious gangsters from Chicago!" To the Nazis, most Americans were gangsters from Chicago.

Commenting on our fighting effect displayed on the Italian front, Sally reported through another special broadcast, ". . . men of the Five Hundred Seventeenth were much better than we anticipated. But . . . you will lose men."

OPERATION DRAGOON—THE PLAN

According to the William Breuer book, *Operation Dragoon*, the 517th originally had been sent to Italy in response to a Seventh Army request for airborne troops to support Operation Anvil. This was to be the invasion of Southern France. Numerous combat teams, including the 517th, had been withdrawn from the line in Italy while invasion air and naval forces began assembling for the assault on the French Riviera.

Renamed from Anvil, Operation Dragoon became the Allied invasion in the South of France on August 15, 1944, and in effect the second European D-Day, which was launched two months after Overlord.

As such, it has been overshadowed by its predecessor, but its significance cannot be underestimated. The operation initially was planned to be executed in conjunction with Operation Overlord, but the lack of available resources led to a cancellation of the second landing.

By July 1944, the landing was reconsidered as the clogged-up ports in Normandy following Overlord's success did not have the capacity to adequately supply the Allied forces. Concurrently, the French high command pushed for a revival of the operation that would include large numbers of French troops.

As a result, the operation finally was approved in July to be executed in August. From strategic decisions made by Allied and Axis high commands to the intelligence war waged by Allied code-breakers, the Germans defeated French resistance forces on the Vergers while individual OSS (Office of Strategic Services) agents on the ground attempted to keep pace with a fast-moving battlefield.

The OSS was a wartime intelligence agency of the United States during World War II. It was the predecessor to the Central Intelligence Agency (CIA), and it aided the Allies in providing critical intelligence to wreak a blitzkrieg-style defeat on the Wehrmacht. This victory removed the lingering memories of the earlier catastrophes of 1940.

EXECUTING THE PLAN

On July 2, 1944, the Allied Combined Chiefs of Staff issued a directive to the commander-in-chief for the Mediterranean to go ahead with Operation Dragoon on August 15. As a result of this directive, the 517th PRCT was released from IV Corps and assigned to the First Airborne Task Force, which was assembling troops, aircraft, ships, and material for the upcoming invasion of southern France.

The German Nineteenth Army was stationed along the Mediterranean coastline in southern France with four divisions and a corps headquarters west of the Rhone River. East of the Rhone is where the Wehrmacht LXII Corps had a division at Draguignan holding Marseilles and Toulon and another division stationed southwest of Cannes. There were an estimated thirty thousand enemy troops in the assault area which was targeted by Operation Dragoon. The Wehrmacht had another two hundred thousand within a few days march.

The US Army planners decided early that an airborne force of division size would be needed. Since a group that large was not available in the Mediterranean at the time, a force of comparable size would have to be improvised. In response, the 517th PRCT, 509th and 551st Parachute Infantry Battalions, and the 550th Airborne

Infantry Battalion were committed.

Other units in Italy were designated *gliderborne,* to be trained by the 550th and the airborne training center. As July wore on, the concentration of airborne forces in the Rome area was almost complete. Two additional troop carrier wings totaling 413 aircraft intended for the parachute drop were sent from England.

The goal of the invasion was to secure the vital ports on the French Mediterranean coast and increase pressure on the German forces by opening another front. After some preliminary commando operations, US VI Corps landed on the beaches of the Côte d'Azur under the shield of a large naval task force, followed by several divisions of French Army B.

They were opposed by the scattered forces of the German Army Group G, which had been weakened by the relocation of portions of its divisions to other fronts along with the replacement of its soldiers with third-rate *Ostlegionen* (eastern legions). Some members of the Ostlegionen units were conscripted—or coerced—into serving; others volunteered. Many were former Soviet personnel recruited from prisoner of war camps.

These troops were frequently stationed away from front lines and used for coastal defense or rear-area activities, such as security operations, thus freeing up regular German forces for front-line service. Outfitted with obsolete equipment, these soldiers were not prepared to halt the coming invasion.

Hindered by Allied air supremacy and a large-scale uprising from the French Resistance, the weak German forces were defeated swiftly. The Germans withdrew to the north through the Rhône Valley to establish a stable defense line at Dijon. Allied mobile units were able to overtake the Germans and partially block their route at the town of Montélimar.

The ensuing battle led to a stalemate, with neither side able to achieve a decisive breakthrough until the Germans finally completed their withdrawal and retreated from the town. While the Germans were retreating, the French managed to capture the important ports of Marseille and Toulon. The Germans were not able to hold Dijon and ordered a complete withdrawal from Southern France.

German Army Group G retreated farther north, pursued by Allied forces. The fighting ultimately came to a stop at the Vosges Mountains, where German Army Group G finally was able to establish a stable defense line. After meeting up with Allied units from Operation Overlord, the Allied forces were in need of reorganizing. Facing stiffened German resistance, the offensive was halted on September 14.

Operation Dragoon was considered a success by the Allies. It enabled them to liberate most of southern France in just four weeks, while inflicting heavy casualties on the German forces—although a substantial number of the best German units were able to escape. The captured French ports were put into operation immediately allowing the Allies to solve their supply problems on the Atlantic coastline.

RIGGERS

Gordon leading his squad

The 517th Parachute Regimental Combat Team was part of the First Airborne Task Force, which had the mission of jumping behind enemy lines in southeastern France for Operation Dragoon on August 15, 1944.

Throughout preparations for this combat jump, it was noted that there was a serious lack of paratrooper helmets available. To alleviate this drawback, standard infantry M1 helmets were specially modified by the unit riggers with the installation of a new chinstrap. The problem facing the 517th's riggers was how to prevent the standard Infantry version of the M-1 helmets they had from coming off the wearer's head during their jump.

517th Camo Helmet

The infantry standard chinstrap was shortened on both sides, and a replacement buckle and makeshift chin cup was sewn into place. The modified chinstrap was designed to fit to the wearers chin as tightly as possible, to avoid losing the helmet during the jump. What makes this helmet modification stand out is how the helmet's chin straps were altered in combination with a distinctive pattern left on the helmet body as a result of having camouflage paint applied to it over a shrimp type netting material.

The 517th Parachute Regimental Combat Team is the only unit of the US Army to have used this type of modified helmet during World War II. The modified helmets can immediately be traced back to the 517th PRCT and Operation Dragoon. Approximately three thousand such helmets were configured, most of which were camouflaged with spray paint, adding to the unique look of these helmets.

BEWARE OF DARKNESS

The date of the invasion was tentatively set for the morning of August 15, 1944, but that would change. The 517th PRCT had been allocated 180 aircraft in four serials. A serial represents a flight of C-47 aircraft numbering three or four dozen planes each.

The combat team was sealed off on August 10, five days before departure. This meant no liberty for the men, and no interaction with anyone outside their units. Maps, escape kits, and invasion scripts were issued and studied. Radio beacons would be used to guide the serials from Elba to the northern tip of Corsica.

From there, radar and Navy beacon ships would lead them to Agay, where each serial would descend to 1,500 feet, slow to 125 miles (knots) per hour, and hone in on its drop zone (DZ) by looking for beacons and lights put out by pathfinder teams on the ground. Each plane carried six equipment bundles in pararacks underneath its belly. These too, were dropped at 125 knots per hour, and the paratroopers would have to locate and retrieve this equipment once they land. As you can imagine, everything didn't go according to plan.

It was a sight that rarely had been seen before. An hour after midnight on August 15, 396 C-47 aircraft, scattered over 150 miles at ten airfields in west-central Italy, began turning over their engines. At ten-second intervals, planes taxied down dirt runways, lifted off, and circled into formation. The dust, compounded by darkness, was so thick that many pilots had to use compass bearings to find their way down the runways.

Takeoff times were from 0136 to 0151 for the ten serials comprising the full jump force, depending on the distance to the first check point at Elba. Each serial required over an hour to get into formation. With nearly 400 aircraft in the sky, heading for southern France, it appeared as a *V of V*'s column with each serial stretching nine planes wide. Four aircraft on the left, four aircraft on the right, with one additional aircraft leading the way. Due to the large number of aircraft, these pilots had to maintain a careful flight discipline in order to not collide with one another and stay on course to their assigned drop zones.

The entire formation, from the head of the first serial to the tail of the last, was more than one hundred miles long. This was the *Albatross* mission (renamed *Operation Dragoon*)—to drop more than 9,000 paratroopers and over one thousand equipment bundles into southern France, while the enemy concentrated deadly fire on the invading force.

In the middle of a war, the best plans of commanders often get disrupted. As the operation began to unfold, most of the pathfinders missed their drop zones. This created immediate problems, because maps carried by most of the troopers were not valid for the area they landed, and they had to figure out how and where to rendezvous while they were busy fighting to stay alive.

North of La Ciotat, aircrews dropped three hundred parachute dummies and a large quantity of rifle simulators which went off in firecracker-like explosions as they hit the ground. This was intended to confuse and distract the enemy.

The four serials bearing the 517th PRCT began drops at 0430. First to arrive was Lt. Col. Dick Seitz' Second Battalion in Serial Six flown by the 440th Group from Ombrone. Lt. Col. Mel Zais' Third Battalion was due next in the 439th Group's Serial Seven from Orbetello. The 460th Field Artillery in Serial Eight with the 437th Group from Montalto fared better than the Third Battalion but not as well as the Second.

Twenty plane loads jumped early and were spread from Fréjus to the west. Last in was Serial Nine at 0453, flown by the 435th Group from Canino with Lt. Col. Boyle's First Battalion and Battery C of the 460th. All told, only about 20 percent of the 517th PRCT landed within two miles of the DZ, and the rest were scattered across the countryside. Once paratroopers hit the ground, they became infantry.

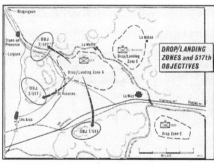

Drop Zones

Within the first eighteen hours, approximately 9,000 troops, 213 artillery pieces, and 221 vehicles, along with many anti-tank guns, had been flown more than 200 miles across the Mediterranean, landing by parachute and glider in enemy-held territory. Despite widely scattered landings, all missions assigned had been accomplished within forty-eight hours. Airborne task force losses included 560 killed, wounded, and missing, and 283 jump and glider casualties.

The password and countersign used in the first hour were

Lafayette and *Democracy*. An alternate for those who might be separated from their outfit for more than twenty-four hours was *Billy* and *The Kid*. A story was told of a British trooper who, failing to remember the countersign when challenged, finally came up with ". . . some fookin' cowboy."

Actions throughout the next three days threw the German Army into a state of pandemonium. Enemy road convoys were attacked, communication lines severed, and German reinforcements were denied access to the beach landing areas. Towns and villages were occupied by the Allies as troopers fought toward their objectives, capturing Le Muy, Les Arcs, La Motte, and Draguignan.

Recently promoted Lt. Col. Boyle and a handful of First Battalion men made a gallant stand at Les Arcs, while remaining elements of the First Battalion captured assigned objectives.

COURAGE UNDER FIRE

Within all of this action, Gordon and his light machine gun platoon attached to the First Battalion, engaged with the enemy while searching for the rally point objective where they were expected to gather. The commendation below outlines the movements of Sgt. Lippman and his team during this action in France, as recounted by Gordon's commanding officer, Captain Lamar A. Tavoian, who signed the commendation. The second half of this same commendation references his actions in the Battle of the Bulge which will be revealed in the following chapter.

> On 15 Aug. 1944, the combat team jumped in southern France and was badly scattered over a huge area. Sgt. Lippman assembled the men in his stick, and headed for the Battalion objective; enroute, Sgt. Lippman's group encountered a German patrol and immediately opened fire. In the ensuing fire fight,

his group received no casualties and reported they killed three of the enemy. As Sgt. Lippman's orders were to get to the objective, he ordered his group to move on and he and two men stayed in position while the rest of the group moved to safety; then, he and the men rejoined the group.

While continuing on to the objective, the group encountered Major Fraser, the First Battalion Executive Officer, who had assembled a group of approximately forty men from the First Battalion. Sgt. Lippman was then ordered to join forces with Major Fraser, to position his machine guns and prepare to defend the Second Battalion Objective. The Second Battalion had been dropped about twenty miles from their DZ and would not be able to reach their objective at the proper time. The group joined forces and helped defend the objective successfully for two days under heavy artillery fire. The Second Battalion arrived and the entire group under Major Fraser joined the First Battalion.

From 27 Sept. to 1 Nov. 1944, the First Battalion occupied defensive positions at Col De Braus, in southern France, at which time the light machine platoon occupied forward positions and during the entire stay, under intense artillery fire, they had to remain constantly on the alert against infiltrating German patrols. This worked an extreme hardship on Sgt. Lippman, who was constructing dugouts and rotating men to rest areas in the rear. His constant supervision kept casualties to a minimum, and he clearly showed his willingness to put his men's safety and welfare before everything else.

Across the field, fighting Germans on another line, Second Battalion pushed through to join with the First Battalion as Germans began amassing their forces on the outskirts of Les Arcs for an all-out counterattack. The Third Battalion completed a forty-kilometer forced march to help consolidate the regiment. The team attacked all assigned German positions, clearing the way for an Allied beach assault with additional teams pushing toward the north.

517th PIR losses included nineteen killed, 126 combat wounded and 137 non-combat related injured.

Effective German opposition within the airhead had ceased through D+3, or D-Day plus three days.

SOUTHERN FRANCE: A DECISIVE ADVANTAGE

As the US VI Corps moved west, the First Airborne Task Force reverted to Seventh Army control and was assigned to protect the Army's eastern flank, while the main forces moved up the Rhone Valley. The British Second Parachute Brigade returned to Italy and was replaced by the First Special Service Force.

Protection of the Army's eastern flank meant moving as far east as practicable and then protecting the best ground available. The initial task force objective was the line between Fayence and La Napoule. The 517th was assigned the left, special service forces assigned to the center and the 509th/551st placed on the right in a narrow strip along the coast.

The Second and Third Battalions of the 517th were charged with the capture of Fayence and Callian. This was accomplished by August 21. Saint-Cézaire fell to Companies G and I on August 22. During the attack, Company G had been pinned down. Company I surged through heavy fire up the mountainous slope to take the objective. For this action, it earned a commendation from Task Force Commander Maj. Gen. Robert T. Frederick.

Saint-Vallier, Grasse, Bouyon, and La Roquette fell in quick succession. During the attack on La Roquette, Company E distinguished itself and received a commendation from General Frederick.

The 517th Parachute Regimental Combat Team's momentum was slowed by a line of enemy fortifications extending from the Maritime Alps to the sea. On September 3, a small force from the PRCT drove into Monaco and liberated it following a US Naval bombardment.

However, the Germans attempted to hold a series of forts at all costs. On September 5, Company D succeeded in taking some high ground near Col de Braus in the midst of heavy fighting. Companies G and H were successful in capturing Col de Braus—a step closer to the heavily defended Sospel Valley.

The First Battalion, supported by the 460th, pressed into Peira Cava. A red-letter day of the campaign occurred when Ventebren and Tete de Lavina were captured by the Second and Third Battalions.

The remainder of September was spent digging defensive positions in and around Peira Cava. The 517th now held a thinly manned fifteen-mile front, using mines and booby traps to take the place of troopers. Attacks ended the month with the roar of artillery duels echoing through the Maritime Alps.

Despite heavy artillery fire, a patrol from Company F pushed into Sospel on September 29. The Germans withdrew as Company B moved up to occupy Mount Agaisen. The siege of Sospel was over after fifty-one days of continuous fighting. Troopers fanned out in pursuit of the enemy, and 517th involvement with the campaign was terminated on November 17, 1944.

After all this fighting, the regiment marched forty-eight kilometers to La Colle, and, on December 6 boarded a train at Antibes for Soissons. From there, the unit rode the rails for rest, relaxation, refitting, and reassignment to XVIII Airborne Corps. It was a breather, albeit a short one, from continuous fighting and marching.

The 517th PRCT suffered more than 500 casualties with 102 men killed in action. On July 15, 1946, long after these battles, the president of the Provisional Government of the French Republic issued Decision Number 247, awarding the French Croix de Guerre to the 517th Parachute Regimental Combat Team.

"There was no development of that period which added more decisively to our advantages or aided us more in accomplishing the final and complete defeat of German forces."

—GENERAL OF THE ARMY DWIGHT D. EISENHOWER

Not two years out of high school and with no diploma, Gordon had led men through combat against battle-hardened Wehrmacht veterans in very fast-moving life-or-death situations. For those efforts he received a battlefield commendation and a promotion. Many on both sides were older than he; he was still a teenager. But he was learning how to keep his men alive, lead them to accomplish their objectives, and remain on the offensive.

CHAPTER 5

BATTLE OF THE BULGE

"THE PATTON MARCH" WAS COMPOSED and conducted by the iconic movie soundtrack composer Jerry Goldsmith for *Patton*, the 1971 Academy Award nominee for Best Music, Original Score. I can't get this theme out of my head as I write this chapter. It is such an inspiring military march that follows the US Third Army riding across Belgium like the cavalry of old to rescue the embattled 101st Airborne troops in Bastogne. But this time, the cavalry was mechanized with tanks, halftracks, howitzers, and a whole Army division, with not a single horse soldier in sight.

"This (Battle of the Bulge) is undoubtedly the greatest American battle of the war, and will, I believe, be regarded as an ever-famous American victory."

—WINSTON CHURCHILL, BRITISH PRIME MINISTER, 1944

TRUTH

Gordon dealt in realities. Truth. Taught by Grandma Swan, he accepted life as it was—the whole drama of life. It was fascinating! His life was unique. His leadership was authentic. The skills that he employed worked well for him, and for those around him. He learned that the fundamental skills of leadership were adapted to work well in any situation—at church, at home, on the battlefield, in the classroom and in his personal relationships with other human beings. Truth and reality were about to get a huge test right before his eyes.

ARDENNES SALIENT

The sentiment at Supreme Headquarters Allied Expeditionary Force in August 1944 was that two-and-a-half months of bitter fighting had brought the end of the war in Europe within sight, almost within reach. The German Army suffered a major defeat on the Normandy coast, was starting to back away from Operation Dragoon in southern France, and was getting pushed out of Italy. The supreme Allied commander, General Dwight Eisenhower, echoed this view when he noted: "The defeat of the German armies is complete, and the only thing now needed . . . is speed."

However, in reality, the war would rage on for almost another year while an overzealous Allied command stumbled into its biggest victory since Normandy over a missed Wehrmacht build up east of the Ardennes. It's too bad that Eisenhower didn't follow his own instincts. Early on, this battle was called the Ardennes Salient. Later on, it came to be more popularly known as *The Battle of the Bulge*.

While defeating the Wehrmacht in Normandy and chasing them out of France, some discord had arisen among the Allied commanders as they crossed the Seine River on their way to Germany. Whereas British Field Marshall Montgomery wanted to concentrate on a single thrust northeastward through Belgium into the heavily industrialized Ruhr Valley (an area vital to Germany's war effort), the US generals argued for continuing to advance eastward through France on a broad front in accordance with the British and American pre-invasion plan.

Eisenhower, by way of compromise, decided on August 23 that Montgomery's drive into Belgium should have the prior claim on resources until Antwerp was captured. Thereafter, the pre-invasion plan would be resumed, with available resources then redirected toward the center.

The Allies' remarkable advance of 350 miles into the heart of the German defense was thus willingly brought to a halt within a few weeks, giving the enemy breathing space and time to regroup.

In early September, the US and British forces had a combined superiority of twenty to one in tanks and twenty-five to one in aircraft over the Germans. But by November 1944, the Germans still held both the Ruhr Valley and the Saarland after collapsing in the west over the previous sixty days.

One or the other of those prizes easily could have been taken by the Allied armies had General Eisenhower not redirected their attention and resources to support Montgomery's plan. The root of the Allied armies' apathy in September was that none of their top planners had anticipated such a complete breakdown of the mighty German Wehrmacht following its defense of Normandy.

The Allied supreme command was therefore not prepared mentally or materially, to exploit that event by rapidly attacking into Germany. The German armies thus gained time to build up their defending forces, with serious consequences both for occupied Europe and postwar political situations on the European continent.

Adolf Hitler still hoped to drive the Allies back, and he adhered to his principle of concentrating on war in the west. Later in 1944, he assembled on the Western German Front all the manpower that had become available as a consequence of his second total mobilization. A decree of October 18 to raise a *Volkssturm* (home guard) for the defense of the Third Reich conscripted all able-bodied men between the ages of sixteen and sixty years of age.

In mid-November, all six Allied armies on the Western Front had launched a general offensive; though the French First Army and the US Seventh Army had reached the Rhine River in Alsace, there were only small gains in other sectors.

Meanwhile, the German defense was being strengthened continuously with reserves hastily moved into place and with freshly raised Volkssturm forces in addition to the troops that had managed to make their way back from France.

The German buildup along the front was progressing faster than that of the Allies, despite Germany's great inferiority of material resources. By contracting the Western Front with less acreage to defend, it became easier for the Wehrmacht to plug the gaps and build a perimeter of resistance to protect the German homeland. In mid-December 1944, the Germans were ready to give the Allied armies a shock by launching a sizable counteroffensive into the Ardennes Forest.

The hilly, forested Ardennes, held on a ninety-mile front by only six American divisions, was considered a quiet sector. American soldiers amused themselves, for example, by shooting wild boar from spotter aircraft. In the Ardennes, routines resembled those on similar sectors in World War I. By day men filled sandbags, strung wire, and strengthened their foxholes. Officers hid their rank bars in order to avoid the attention of enemy snipers.

Nights were more dangerous and filled with sudden, savage mortar and artillery bombardments and aggressive patrolling in search of prisoners for interrogation by intelligence officers. Probing skirmishes and annoying cannonades, but nothing more.

Both armies appeared resolved to hunker down and camp for the winter.

This was the Ardennes, which Petrarch had described six centuries earlier as "the savage and inhospitable forests from which warriors and armies emerge at great risk." Although the Ardennes was considered the graveyard of military ambition, an unforgiving and inhospitable terrain, it had in fact witnessed many successful military operations.

Through the first half of the twentieth century alone, the Germans had successfully exploited the region twice, during WWI (called the *war to end all wars* at the time) in 1914, and the earlier WWII blitzkrieg in 1940, when the German armies successfully invaded Belgium and France.

German military strength in May 1940 amounted to some 3.5 million men, more than 5,500 aircraft, and ten Panzer divisions. German troops overran Belgium, the Netherlands, Luxembourg, and France in six weeks, starting in May 1940. The Allies defended with less than 2 million men, about a thousand aircraft, and an unequal but comparable number of tanks. So, the German Wehrmacht had done this before. Adolph Hitler presumed they could do it again.

Nevertheless, in 1944, the legend of the Ardennes' impenetrability, especially in the depths of winter, exercised a powerful influence and somehow satisfied the Allies that it was safe to sit tight and prepare for a spring offensive, while waiting on Field Marshall Montgomery's push in the north to conclude. This was a political decision that proved to be costly and almost disastrous for the Allies.

Back in the autumn of 1944, supreme Allied headquarters had deemed the Ardennes a secondary front, reinforcing the north and south with the bulk of American and British forces. Up north, the British and Americans fought their way through a maze of grimly defended positions in hilly country scarred with refuse from mines and industrial sites, furnaces, and dreary industrial towns.

When the US Ninth Army's offensive slithered to a halt in the snows of December, it had penetrated the Western Front to a depth of only ten miles at a cost of 1,333 killed, 6,864 wounded, and 2,059 missing. Thousands more had succumbed to pneumonia and trench foot, as well as combat exhaustion.

Casualties were also high in the north. General Patton's Third Army in the south found the going tough in Lorraine, where he was opposed by Wehrmacht Army Group G, commanded by General Hermann Balck, an accomplished professional officer. Here were two heavyweight fighters going toe-to-toe in a pitched tank battle, with both sides running precariously low on fuel.

In mid-December Gen. Dwight D. Eisenhower, the supreme commander of the Allied Expeditionary Force, had at his disposal forty-eight divisions distributed along a six hundred-mile (nearly one thousand kilometer) front between the North Sea and Switzerland. For the site of their counteroffensive, the Germans chose the hilly and wooded country of the Ardennes. Because it was generally regarded as difficult terrain, a large-scale offensive there was likely to be unexpected. At the same time, the thick woods provided concealment for the massing of forces, whereas the high ground offered a drier surface for the maneuvers of tanks. An awkward feature from an offensive point of view, however, was the fact that the high ground was intersected with deep valleys where the through roads became bottlenecks potentially blocking a tank advance. The goals of the German counteroffensive were far-reaching. They sought to break through to Antwerp, Belgium, by an indirect move then cut off the British Army group from American forces and from its supplies—all designed to lead to a crushing defeat for the isolated British. Overall command of the offensive was given to Field Marshal Gerd von Rundstedt.

Recall that combat operations for the 517th Parachute Regimental Combat Team (PRCT) had ceased in southern France and the PRCT had ridden the rails up through the Maritime Alps into Soissons, France, for a little rest, relaxation, and refitting during late November and early December.

All elements of the PRCT were quartered in Soissons by December 10. Every American airborne unit in Europe was now part of General Matthew B. Ridgway's XVIII Airborne Corps. This included the 82nd and 101st Airborne divisions just back from Montgomery's folly in the Netherlands, the 517th, and 506th, plus other separate units up from the Mediterranean.

Additionally, the US Army 17th Airborne Division in England was preparing to come across to France in the near future. At this time, the 517th was recuperating, repairing equipment, engaging in normal training, and enjoying some relaxation at United Services Organizations (USO) canteens in Soissons.

Farther east in the Ardennes, now a defensive front line, relaxed GIs stationed in the sector were able to enjoy a time out from war. Periodically relaxing on a forty-eight-hour pass at the army's dozen rest centers in Luxembourg and Belgium, they could enjoy a hot shower, drink watered down beer, watch newsreels and Hollywood films.

USO entertainers were occasional guests, as some of the big names from back home came to entertain the men. The arrival of Marlene Dietrich in December was eagerly awaited. Bob Hope USO shows always entertained, as Hope loved to make 'em laugh. Beer and ice cream were available in the towns to the rear.

On December 15, Private Joe Schectman wrote his parents with this ominous note: "We are billeted as comfortably and safely as we were in England. Of course, there's no telling how long I'll be in this paradise. But as long as I am, I'll be safe."

One day later, at half-past five in the morning, Private Schectman and his platoon found themselves drawn into the thick of a major German offensive—which the Allied Generals' staff planners completely missed.

It speaks volumes on the low priority given to the Ardennes that such a critical sector was so sparsely defended by this part of the Allied defense.

In the village of Hosingen, an American observation post sentry atop a concrete water tower on Skyline Drive phoned his company commander to report: "There's a big Kraut column coming, Colonel! They've got tanks and half-tracks and armored cars—everything—and there's a helluva lot of them. It looks like the whole German army!"

HOLDING THE LINE

Drawing from both Sgt. Lippman's after-action report and Army records of the battles, this is perhaps the most arduous stretch of a long trail to Germany—the opening days of the *Ardennes Salient*, as the men on the ground would call it, or the *Battle of the Bulge* as it later came to be known.

The 517th Parachute Regimental Combat Team's First Battalion eventually would fight to aid in halting the fanatical advance of Marshall von Rundstedt's counter-offensive. This brief narrative does not cover the entire period of the Battle of the Bulge, nor the courageous actions of other Allied units engaged in breaking this German push, but only that battle against von Rundstedt's force on the offensive north of Bastogne. The 517th cleared the Soy-Hotton Road during the earliest days of the Bulge, as the crow flies twenty-one miles northwest of Bastogne, which was just one critical objective during the opening days.

From a strategic outlook the Allies were intent on defending the roads leading out of the Ardennes and into Belgium. In response to the German offensive, Allied infantry and tanks swarmed into the sector to defend the seven roads converging through Bastogne. It is here that the famed Easy Company, known as the "Band of Brothers," made their seven-day stand in the late December snows and bitter cold of 1944.

Gordon's eye-witness report of the 517th's actions attacking the Soy-Hotton Road farther north is valuable and intermingled with various complementary reports on the overall battle, participants, and results.

During the night of December 15–16, the German Army launched its last great blitzkrieg offensive of World War II, striking with three armies against weak American positions in the Ardennes region of Belgium and Luxembourg. Allies were taken totally by surprise as German troops pushed their main effort with the Sixth SS and Fifth Panzer Armies, while their Seventh Army on the left made a limited holding attack.

On December 18, the 517th Regiment was alerted by XVIII Airborne Corps command to be prepared to move on a two-hour notice. The regiment remained on an alert status through the next two days.

During a high-level command conference in Verdun called by General Eisenhower on December 19, Eisenhower told his commanders, ". . . the enemy must never be allowed to cross the Meuse. Our weakest spot is in the direction of Namur." Eisenhower explained: "The general plan is to plug the holes in the north and launch a coordinated attack from the south."

DECEMBER 21, 1944

Movement orders finally came at 1100 on December 21, attaching one battery of the 460th and a platoon of the 596th to each rifle battalion. A hole was beginning to open up north of Bastogne along the Soy-Hotton Road, and it needed to be plugged, so the 517th was pulled out of reserve and ordered to take up an aggressive position on the line.

Orders were received through XVIII Airborne Corps command, which directed the 1st Battalion to report to the 3rd Armored Division sector near Soy, Belgium, 164 miles away. Pressure from German armor had made the situation so fluid that it was impossible to tell exactly where the front line began. Company D was immediately attached to the 3rd Armored's Task Force Kane, which held a key defensive position on which the front hinged. Companies A and B detrucked northeast of Soy and were ordered to attack along the highway leading southwest from Soy to Hotton.

The mission of the 1st Battalion was to take the commanding high ground around Haid-Hits, then remove the enemy from Sur-Les-Hys. The main objective was to break through the German line and free surrounded elements of the American 3rd Armored Division in Hotton, Belgium.

While the 1st Battalion was attached to the 3rd Armored, the balance of the 517th was kept busy. The morning after the long truck-ride into Belgium, Company G was detailed as a security force for the XVIII Airborne Corps Command Post. The 517th (minus

1st Battalion and Company G) was attached to the 30th Infantry Division, near Malmedy, where just days before German SS troops massacred a large number of American prisoners of war from the 285th Field Artillery Observation Battalion. The 517th went into battle with this knowledge.

Departing Soissons at 1800 on the evening of December 21, the 1st Battalion motor convoy had orders to proceed to Namur, Belgium, where further orders would be issued. Eager to get into the fight, the battalion commander, Lt. Col. "Wild Bill" Boyle, preceded the battalion, and at Namur, received orders to take his men to Soy and report to the commander of the 3rd Armored Division, Major General Maurice Rose.

CHAPTER 6

SOY-HOTTON ROAD

DECEMBER 22, 1944

The battalion convoy arrived at Namur around 0400 on December 22 and the battalion executive officer received orders from XVIII Corp Airborne command to move the battalion to the vicinity of Soy, where Lt. Col. Boyle would meet them. Three trucks were missing from the convoy, having dropped out because of motor troubles and instructions were left to have these trucks proceed to Soy following their repairs.

Charley Company proceeded to the 3rd Armored Division Command Post and reported to Major General Rose. Very little information could be obtained from staff officers, except that the situation remained vague as the advance of the German forces had not yet been checked.

At four that afternoon, the main battalion force detrucked in the wooded area northeast of Soy, where the 3rd Armored Division command post was located and had been under daily heavy and continuous artillery fire.

Lt. Col. Boyle had learned the following information: the towns of Marche and La-Roche had been engulfed by German Armor. Hotton was manned by 3rd Armored HQ troops and had been bypassed and surrounded by the enemy. German armor was probing a salient toward Liege, astride the two main highways leading north.

There was no contact on the right with the 84th Infantry Division, nor on the left with the 82nd Airborne Division. The 82nd was holding Soy and Hotton with depleted forces which had momentarily stopped the Germans in their tracks.

The battalion was ordered immediately to attack along the highway leading southwest from Soy to Hotton. At this point Gordon, a staff sergeant leading his light machine gun platoon, joined Able Company. The gravity of the situation was so severe that no rest could be considered because there had been trouble in the area for the previous twenty-four hours. No time could be used to prepare a hot meal, or to rest or relax from the long overnight road trip.

The battalion moved over the north-south road through Soy, crossing the line of departure and jumping off in the attack toward the Germans surrounding Hotton.

Effective strength of the battalion present at this time was down from the original 800 to 32 officers and 454 enlisted men, nearly half were lost in five months to casualties and disease.

Six officers and 117 enlisted men of Charley Company had been detached and reported to General Rose at Treynean for security duty.

Enemy forces had cut the Soy-Hotton highway in half and were well dug in among the woods covering the road. They were also on the commanding high ground around Haid-Hits.

With all that, the 1st Battalion mission was to capture the commanding ground at Haid-Hits and at Sur-Les-Hys, clear the woods on each side of the road, establish an MLR (main line of resistance) between Soy and Hotton, and break through to the 3rd Armored Division garrison surrounded in Hotton.

For this mission the troopers would be well prepared. Standing operating procedure dictated that each rifleman carried at least three hundred rounds of ammunition. Machine gun crews were to transport at least eight hundred rounds of linked ammunition, and every man was to have no less than two grenades. There were to be at least two light assault weapons per squad and five to six smoke grenades in each platoon. Every soldier was to carry two C Ration meals and a canteen of water, as well as an ample supply of entrenching tools. What they didn't have was an adequate supply of winter clothing.

The crew-served weapons personnel also carried carbines.

The battalion normally would have three medics per rifle company and a battalion aid section, along with a communications platoon, but battle casualties thinned those ranks.

The battalion moved out, with Able Company leading and Baker Company echeloned to the left. The remnants of Charley Company were used as a reserve force. Lt. Col. Boyle directed Baker Company's 1st Platoon on the left with 2nd Platoon on the right. He told both platoon leaders to advance abreast, and positioned 3rd Platoon behind the 1st as a reserve.

Second Platoon got ahead of 1st Platoon's position after crossing the jump off point. An enemy force of platoon size was encountered, which attacked both flanks with small arms fire. Pinned down and suffering casualties, and attempting to relieve the pressure, 2nd Platoon tried to establish contact with the 1st Platoon's right flank.

Anxious to develop the situation, the 1st Platoon leader maneuvered his twenty-seven-man force in that direction. A few minutes later, the point of 2nd Platoon bumped into a squad of German soldiers moving toward them along a well-used trail, which was parallel to the platoon's direction of advance.

Headquarters Company's 81mm mortar platoon went into position and immediately started receiving enemy fire raining in from machine gun emplacements. That trajectory fire was from an estimated six self-propelled guns and possible tank fire. Artillery and mortar fire fell over the entire area.

Lt. Col. Boyle ordered Baker Company to move across the road to the south, then deploy and attack on the left flank. Baker, in the action to follow, reduced two machine gun positions and killed or drove out a platoon of enemy from positions but drew an attack from six German Tiger tanks. Gordon wrote, "One tank was knocked out and the others were forced into retirement. The reason is not apparent, as the heavy armor was impenetrable to our rocket launcher. The one damaged tank resulted from a lucky hit."

Weather for the period was freezing, with snow flurries. Up to this point, the battalion had moved only a short distance because the terrain was bare of trees and the ground was only gently sloping, affording practically no cover or concealment.

DECEMBER 23, 1944

At about half past midnight, Lt. Col. Boyle determined that a frontal assault on the excellent German positions would be a needless waste of time and life. He was granted permission to take Able Company into Hotton by the road leading through the French town of Ny. Four medium tanks and six half-tracks were placed at his disposal.

Two Platoons of Able Company, along with the section of LMG (light machine guns) mounted on vehicles for the movement, prepared to move out, with Staff Sergeant Lippman leading this heavily armed unit. The remainder of the battalion, under the command of the executive officer, Major Fraser, was dispersed in the following manner: Charley Company, with thirty-two men, was sent to the high ground to protect five Allied tanks that were concealed in a position north of the road. Baker and one platoon of Able Company moved into position for the assault.

All were to be prepared to launch a coordinated attack toward Hotton to meet up with Boyle's forces that were moving through Hotton and back up the road to attack the Germans from the rear. With the enemy drawn to the south of the attack by Baker it was thought that Boyle's task force would meet only light resistance on the northern road through Ny, and the plan was based on this expectation.

In the skirmishes that followed, Sgt. Lippman's commanding officer commended him for his exemplary actions. This is the second half of his battlefield commendation from his commanding officer. The first half, which was previously covered in the Operation Dragoon chapter, describes Gordon's accomplishments in the southern France combat jump.

EXCERPT OF GORDON'S BATTLEFIELD COMMENDATION:

Tech. Sgt. Gordon J. Lippman has been a member of Hq. Co. 1st. Bn. since the regiment was organized, and has distinguished himself in every action. His courage as light machine gun platoon Sgt., and platoon leader during combat in Italy, France, Belgium, and Germany, has been outstanding.

The Battalion was ordered to attack at once and clear the road from Soy to Hotton, and also to clear Hotton. Half of the town was held by MP's and cooks from the Third Armored division, and the other half by the Germans. The first attempt to clear this road failed. The Battalion CO then decided that Company B, of the 1st Battalion, would continue the attack to Hotton and he, the Battalion Commander, would take Company A, mounted on tanks and halftracks, and try to get into Hotton from a rear route.

The machine gun platoon was attached to Company A for this action and as the Platoon Leader was absent, Sgt. Lippman commanded the Platoon. Company A managed to get into Hotton and attack toward Soy. Sgt. Lippman and six machine gunners were with the attacking platoon. They cleared part of the town. Sgt. Lippman then set his machine gunners in the captured buildings and held for the rest of the night.

The next day, Company B cleared the road from Soy and joined Company A in Hotton. The town was in our hands. Hotton was under heavy enemy shelling and small arms fire during the attack, all of which took place at night. Throughout this operation and the others mentioned (earlier), Sgt. Lippman has shown an extremely high sense of dedication to duty, and clearly exhibited his ability to command troops in combat.

It is the firm belief of the undersigned, that Technical Sergeant Lippman has demonstrated his ability to command both in garrison and actual combat, under fire, as cited in the above-mentioned instances. Technical Sergeant Lippman is considered worthy of a commission from the standpoint of value to the service in future assignments.

Lt. Col. Boyle's task force rolled quickly through Ny, and soon began receiving sporadic but ineffective enfilade small arms fire from an enemy position on the south of the town. To the right and farther downhill was the 3rd Platoon, with all three squads on the line and machine guns on the flanks. Although enemy soldiers could no longer be seen, he knew that they were somewhere in front of him. He was about to give the signal to continue when men in his 3rd squad spotted about twenty Germans scrambling toward two large hills off the platoon's left flank.

On the north of Hotton, the force received sudden and heavy 20mm fire from a German outpost, which was quickly dispatched by Allied tanks and paratroopers manning the half-track mounted machine guns.

Boyle then pushed in to relieve the besieged garrison of Hotton at daylight on December 23. As they sought to wheel and return to Soy, they were held up by German armored infantry, which held command of the houses in the east side of town and had erected a brick wall across the road leading back to Soy.

At the same time, the American-held west end of town was receiving artillery fire from German guns across the river to the southeast. The narrow streets walled in by houses on both sides made defense by the Germans easy and attacks by Boyle's task force extremely difficult.

A house-to-house campaign was initiated to engage the enemy with substantial force and fire at close range. This diverted German attention from the remainder of the battalion and taught Gordon a valuable lesson he would utilize in future skirmishes.

Meanwhile, Task Force Fraser, along with five medium tanks, attacked toward Hotton along the Soy-Hotton railroad. German high-velocity self-propelled guns that had been used as anti-personnel guns the previous night opened up from wooded positions to the southwest, and within a few minutes six of the Sherman tanks were knocked out. At the same time, heavy mortar concentrations laid down by the Germans further wounded tankmen and supporting troopers.

The entire remaining task force regrouped in the woods and resumed their determined push south through the wooded area along the railroad. Here, they walked through extremely thick undergrowth, not suitable for tanks, so the remaining tanks had to return to the vicinity of Soy.

Throughout the second night of continued fighting, the Fraser Task Force pressed its attack through incredibly dense undergrowth, scrub cedar, and shrubbery that limited visibility often to ten yards and never more than thirty yards.

DECEMBER 24, 1944

In the company of heroes, Gordon was united in battle with many of his teammates from Camp Toccoa, men of the 517th PIR who had fought together in Italy and Southern France. They had been joined by replacements brought up from the rear. Now in the thick of one of the most pivotal battles of the European War, they were engaged in life-and-death struggles, fighting for every inch of ground—battle hardened veterans along with men tasting combat for the first time.

More than 80 percent of these men died on European soil. It was an overwhelming loss, but the survivors had to fight on. In the midst of these skirmishes, troopers stuck together, covered each other's backs and put their own lives on the line to win the battle and live another day.

Foot by foot, inch by inch, toward the German border they fought to seize the advantage. Private First-Class (PFC) Bud Biddle was one of those valiant warriors, fighting alongside Gordon's platoon as it advanced toward Hotton. Biddle would eventually become the regiment's only Medal of Honor awardee.

Melvin "Bud" Biddle was in Reims, France on December 16, scheduled to go home when the Germans launched their attack. A veteran of campaigns in Italy and southern France, he had turned in his equipment and was idly passing the time listening to Axis Sally when the news broke about the German attacks. He was more amused than influenced by her show.

That night, she announced, "The men of the 517th Parachute Infantry Regiment think you're going home but you're not." Biddle would soon find himself back on the line in Belgium. Joining the regiment on the Soy-Hotton Road, Biddle quickly found himself in the thick of the same fight Gordon was in, trying to hold the line against a sudden and massive German mechanized onslaught.

The men no longer going home were issued new equipment, so new, in fact, that their rifles were still packed in Cosmoline (thick, firm, waxy) grease, which the men had to clean off before they boarded trucks and joined the rest of the PRCT at a crossroads in the area near the most advanced point of the German army. There they faced Panzer divisions, paratroops, and SS soldiers attacking in force. The mission, as stated above, was to clear the Germans out of three miles of territory on the road between the towns of Soy and Hotton.

Biddle was a lead scout for the 517th, a job he had inherited when other scouts were wounded or killed during the Italian campaign. One of his qualifications for this role was his superb vision. "I saw every German out in front before they saw me, which was a large part of keeping me alive," he said in *Above and Beyond: A History of the Medal of Honor from the Civil War to Vietnam.*

He was keenly aware of the responsibility he held as the lead scout and said later it helped him forget his fear. "I think I got so I would rather die than be a coward. I was terrified most of the time but there were two or three times when I had no fear. It's remarkable. It makes it so you can operate in the lead."

Biddle was ahead of his company as it crawled through thick underbrush toward railroad tracks leading out of Hotton. Unseen by the enemy, he crawled to within ten feet of three sentries. Firing with his M1 rifle, he wounded one man in the shoulder and killed a second with two shots near the heart. The third sentry fled, but not before Biddle shot him twice. "I should have got him. He kept running and alerted their machine guns, then all hell broke loose."

Under heavy fire from several machine guns, Biddle stayed on point as his unit crawled to within range, lobbed grenades and destroyed all but one of the guns. With his last grenade, Biddle blew up the remaining machine gun. Then he charged the surviving gunners and eliminated them all.

That night, the Americans heard a large number of vehicles, which Biddle first thought had to be American: "I'd never heard so many Germans speaking English. (But) they didn't have equipment like we had, not in numbers." Biddle volunteered to lead two others in a scouting foray to make contact with these "Americans."

Searching through the darkness, the three men came upon a German officer who fired at them. Scrambling for cover and separated from the other two, Biddle crawled toward the German lines by mistake. Realizing his error, he continued to reconnoiter alone and carried back valuable information to be used in the next day's attack.

The next morning, Biddle spotted a group of Germans dug in along a ridge. He ducked behind a small bank for cover but found that he could not properly maneuver to shoot. During his basic training back at Camp Toccoa, Biddle had learned to shoot from a sitting position but at the time he thought that there would be no way to use it in combat. Under combat conditions, he moved into a sitting stance and shot fourteen men. He hit each one in the head, imagining that the helmets were the same as the targets he had aimed at in training.

Although others in his unit later went to view the bodies, Biddle could not bring himself to look on the carnage he had wrought. His sharpshooting, however, made it possible for his unit to advance and secure the village.

Biddle was wounded a few days later when a German 88mm artillery shell exploded against a building behind him. As he was returning to his unit from a hospital in London sometime later, another soldier asked him if he had heard about "that guy in the Bulge who shot all those people. My God, between Soy and Hotton it was littered with Germans. I think they're going to put that guy in for the Medal of Honor." Pfc. Biddle was presented his Medal of Honor after the war, by President Harry Truman, for his courageous actions along the Soy-Hotton Road.

Back in the wooded area, Task Force Fraser had 187 officers and men from three companies. Their attack continued throughout the night with every inch of the area fanatically defended by German fire teams in excellently prepared positions. Enemy strength was later determined to be a reinforced company in this area.

All of the positions were overrun and the defenders killed in position as they stood their ground. A manifestation of the excellent morale and determined resistance of the enemy showed up soon as German machine gunners started shouting loudly, "Merry Christmas, American bastards," as they fired long bursts at the attacking Americans.

Although this German gesture was meant to disrupt the attack, it greatly antagonized and encouraged the troopers, for many had not realized it was Christmas Eve. Someone had to pay for these miserable conditions. In the end, fifty enemy soldiers lost their lives in those foxholes and the remaining Germans beat a hasty retreat back to new positions closer to Hotton.

Capitalizing on this bloody success, the Fraser Task Force regrouped at 0600 on December 24, brought up two medium tanks, and moved out. Two enemy tanks spotted and immediately wheeled on the force to open fire but were knocked out by American Sherman tanks before either German Tiger commander could get their guns trained.

The task force continued on the north side of the road to Hotton, hampered by many snipers, and hastily formed a defensive group of squad strength. Advancing toward Hotton with matching fire, all resistance along the road folded up and two self-propelled guns, which fired on the Boyle force in Hotton, were knocked out. The supporting Wehrmacht infantry began to flee badly in disarray.

By 1130, Task Force Fraser had joined Task Force Boyle in the outskirts of Hotton, relieving most of the pressure on the beleaguered garrison they came to rescue.

At 1230, after hastily eating K-rations, weary from two days and two nights of continuous fighting in the freezing weather, the entire force pushed off to further clear the Soy-Hotton highway.

While the enemy was still reeling and disorganized, they did not stand to fight due to the overwhelming 1st Battalion force attack. The battalion overran the high ground at Sur-Les-Hys, and with this commanding overlook of Hotton, the Americans controlled the critical road network there.

One company and a platoon of another company were left to occupy Sur-Les-Hys, setting up a main line of resistance (MLR) and defending it against possible counterattack from the south. A Panzer division was detected enroute to the town of Hotton from the south but was intercepted by the American 84th Division before it could get there.

At the road junction of Haid-Hits, six German tankmen, fighting as infantry, were captured. Baker Company was further assigned the mission of establishing a roadblock at this point. The enemy who had escaped these skirmishes had withdrawn to the vicinity of Werdin.

The remainder of the battalion (two platoons of Able Company and one platoon of Charley Company) returned to Soy. This group of the 1st Battalion was then placed in reserve, along with the 290th Infantry Regiment, 75th Division, which had just been attached to the battalion.

The Headquarters Company 81mm mortar platoon moved into Soy, half of the LMG platoon was attached to Baker Company and provided the main line of resistance. It was here that these men received their first warm meal since departing Soissons three days earlier.

The German Army drive into the north had been stopped. The US Airborne forces in Hotton had been relieved. Enemy elements between Soy and Hotton had been destroyed and the high ground had been captured. A stable line of resistance had been established from which an attack to the south could be launched.

The mission of the 1st Battalion had been completely accomplished over continuous and tireless fighting covering the previous seventy-two hours.

Total casualties since beginning of action included eight officers and ninety-three enlisted men. The weather was freezing, with zero visibility. It's remarkable the casualties were so low.

The 1st Battalion took a well-deserved breather, holding the line it had established. The 290th Infantry Regiment, 75th Division prepared to attack toward the south.

DECEMBER 25, 1944

Just prior to midnight, the 290th Infantry pushed off in a night attack from the Soy-Hotton MLR manned by Baker Company, reinforced with half of the LMG Platoon.

Two battalions of the 290th attacked abreast southward with objectives on the high ground at La Roumiere Ol Fagne and the nearby town of Wy. The first battalion of the 290th was assigned to the right objective and the second battalion was assigned the left objective.

This regiment was receiving its baptism of fire, facing the zealously inspired troops of Marshal von Rundstedt in bitter cold weather, with snow flurries. The Americans had two strikes against them before they crossed the line of departure.

Nearly twelve hours later, at noon on Christmas Day, Lt. Col. Boyle was informed that the left battalion had all but taken the town of Wy, but that the right battalion had failed to accomplish its mission. The 290th Regimental Reserve Battalion failed to reach its objective to rescue 1st Battalion and was badly disorganized.

Lt. Col. Boyle received orders to attack and take the objective at La Roumiere Ol Fagne. His remaining forces consisted of Able Company with thirty men, Charley Company with twenty-one men and twenty-two men of the LMG Platoon, with Sgt. Lippman leading the last group.

The 81mm mortar platoon went into position the night before to support the MLR, so it remained in position. It was vitally essential for Baker Company to remain in its present position on the MLR. Lt. Col. Boyle made plans to attack the enemy position on the right flank with Able Company. Charley Company was to provide support.

The two battalions of the 290th were somewhere in the area north of the objective. In the fog of battle, it was erroneously reported that all soldiers of the 290th who reached the objective had been killed.

Jumping off at 1400 that afternoon, 1st Battalion, 517th moved through the thickly wooded approaches from the northeast, preceded by covering artillery fire. Initial progress was slow as the high ground was approached, due to intense small arms fire from enemy machine guns, rifles, and a high proportion of machine pistols.

Realizing that being pinned down would also invite enemy mortar fire, the men charged across the Lisbelle stream and up the slope through intense fire. They engaged with the enemy close enough for a wide use of hand grenades. The battalion suffered the loss of 46 men during this engagement but slashed through and folded up the enemy positions facing them. The battalion outflanked the Germans by 1730 and seized the objective, patrolling forward.

At dusk, the men of the first battalion once again had achieved their objective, and the enemy had been annihilated.

Information from prisoners who were captured revealed that the objective had been occupied by a reinforced German battalion. An exact count of enemy cannot be quoted, as the first battalion was relieved the following morning before a count could be made.

The entire enemy battalion, as near as could be determined, was completely destroyed. The tenacity of the German soldier can be measured by the fact that not more than fifteen prisoners from battalion strength had been taken by all of the attacking forces, and none of the occupying enemy forces escaped.

On Christmas Day, the PRCT was released and returned to XVIII Airborne Corps control.

The early part of Christmas night was spent patrolling in the wooded area, on the forward slopes, to eradicate the remaining scattered enemy troops. On this night, Lt. Col. Boyle was placed in command of all the troops on the objective, including the two battalions of the 290th Infantry.

Lt. Col. Boyle, with his staff and officers, oriented each of the company commanders of the 290th, assisted them in reorganization, and placed them in defensive positions along the south edge of the woods on the objective.

DECEMBER 26, 1944

At 0600 on the morning of December 26, as one of the companies was moving into position, a German counterattack was launched from the south, estimated at platoon size. It was completely routed, with fifteen killed and four prisoners taken and no American losses. Enemy artillery bombarded the hill throughout the remaining time that the first battalion occupied the position.

Elsewhere, the fall of Manhay to the II SS Panzer Corps on Christmas Day sent shock waves throughout the Allied Command. From Manhay the Germans could continue north toward Liege or turn against the flank of the 3rd Armored and the 82nd Airborne.

General Ridgeway was ordered to retake Manhay at all costs. The directive to recapture Manhay arrived in the PRCT Command Post at 1400 on December 26. One battalion of the 517th was attached to the 7th Armored Division for this mission.

The 3rd Battalion (minus Company G) under Lt. Col. Forest S. Paxton was given the assignment. One platoon of the 596th Engineers and a section of the regimental demolitions platoon was attached. The battalion would cross two miles of snow-covered terrain in darkness, before reaching the line of departure. The attack commenced at 0215, after a ten-minute barrage by eight battalions of American artillery.

The attack proceeded as planned after five thousand artillery rounds pummeled the area in four concentrations, and by 0330, the last pocket of resistance was eliminated. A German counterattack thirty minutes later was driven off. The 3rd Battalion suffered thirty-six casualties, sixteen killed and twenty wounded.

At 0800 the next morning, 1st Battalion started to retrieve the 290th on the hill. This was completely accomplished by 1600. The battalion then was reassembled from its position on the MLR Soy-Hotton highway and marched back to Soy.

Mission accomplished.

SUMMARY

The 1st Battalion, 517th Parachute Infantry Combat Team, called to action as the German offensive gained momentum, established a stable main line of resistance on a six-thousand-yard front (that's sixty football fields laid out end-to-end) between Soy and Hotton. In accomplishing its mission, the 1st Battalion fought for the greater share of three days and nights in bitter cold weather with no sleep and a meager amount of K rations.

They stopped an obsessively advancing enemy, drove them from their sector, relieved the beleaguered town of Hotton, and on the fourth day, were further committed in a critical situation, threatening to neutralize all it had accomplished.

The 517th achieved a mission in which two battalions ahead of them had tried and failed to achieve an objective—and the 517th did it with less than a full complement of men.

For its victory, the unit paid a dear price of 150 wounded and 11 men killed, but in doing so, accounted for at least 210 enemy dead. They also took eighteen prisoners and knocked out three tanks, nine self-propelled guns, a half track, an armored recon car, *Volksgrenadiers* (the name given specialized German professional military troops, who were equipped with submachine guns and other effective weapons and equipment), and an ammunition truck. For its service in the Soy-Hotton mission, 1st Battalion was awarded the Presidential Distinguished Unit Citation.

CONTINUING BATTLE OF THE BULGE ACTION

Early on New Year's Day, the PRCT was attached to the 82nd Airborne and alerted to go on the attack. On January 3, 1945, the PRCT, acting as the left flank of the 82nd, attacked south along the Salm River. The 551st PIR, as an attached unit, fought through Basse-Bodeux, while the 2nd Battalion of the 517th captured Trois-Ponts.

The southerly attack continued to Mont-de-Fosse where early arrivers were subjected to intense shelling.

The 1st Battalion moved through ground already captured to seize Saint-Jacques and Bergeval. The 3rd Battalion continued its attack across the Salm River and moved to the east. On January 9, they circled around the 551st and closed on the bank of the Salm at Petit-Halleux.

That night, advance elements of the 75th Infantry Division arrived to make arrangements for relieving the 82nd in the area. To get them off to a good start, 3rd Battalion, 517th under direction of the 504th, crossed the Salm and seized Grand Halleux.

The 1st Battalion relieved the 112th Infantry at Stavelot, along the northern bank of the Ambleve, by January 12.

A new attack was launched at 0800 on the morning of January 13 to seize a line running from Spineux, north of Grand Halleux, to Poteaux, eight miles south of Malmedy. Combat operations continued pushing the front eastward until the capture of St. Vith, which was another strategic objective of the US Army.

The Battle of the Bulge, the final great German offensive of WWII, had been repulsed in forty-one days of bloody warfare with extensive casualties on both sides.

As a result, Western Allied offensive plans were delayed by five or six weeks. But the German offensive had exhausted its resources on the Western Front. The German collapse opened the way for the Allies to ultimately break the Siegfried Line, which at one time was considered to be impenetrable.

The war in Europe essentially had been won, but the enemy continued to fight desperately for another six months before surrendering.

THE RHINE RIVER CROSSING

In mid-December General Eisenhower wrote to Ernie Pyle, the well-known war correspondent, that it was his foot soldiers who had demonstrated the "real heroism—which is the uncomplaining acceptance of unendurable conditions." At Aachen, at Metz, in the Hürtgen Forest, in the Vosges Mountains, along the length of the Siegfried Line, and on to the Rhine River, the Allied infantryman had persevered and, through their determination, vanquished the Wehrmacht.

Early on New Year's Day, the PRCT was attached to the 82nd Airborne and alerted to go on the attack. On January 3, the PRCT, acting as the left flank of the 82nd, attacked south along the Salm River. The 551st Parachute Infantry, as an attached unit, fought through Basse Bodeux, while Second Battalion captured Trois Ponts. The southerly attack continued to Monte Fosse, where advance elements were subjected to intense shelling.

The 1st Battalion moved through ground already taken to seize Saint Jacques and Bergeval. The 3rd Battalion continued its attack across the Salm River and moved to the east. On January 9, they circled around the 551st and closed on the bank of the Salm at Petit-Halleux. That night, advance details of the 75th Infantry Division arrived to make arrangements for relieving the 82nd in the area. To get them off to a good start, 3rd Battalion, 517th—under direction of the 504th—crossed the Salm and seized Grand Halleux.

Colonel Graves received orders on January 11 that the PRCT (minus 2nd Battalion, attached to the 7th Armored Division) was attached to the 106th Infantry Division. The immediate job was to relieve the 112th Infantry at Stavelot and along the northern bank of the Ambleve. This was accomplished by the 1st Battalion on January 12.

A new attack was launched at 0800 on the morning of January 13, to seize a line running from Spineux, north of Grand Halleux, to Poteaux, eight miles south of Malmedy. The 1st and 2nd Battalions moved to the south capturing Butay, Lusnie, Henumont, Coulee, and Logbierme and established blocks at Petit Thier and Poteaux. The PRCT had now reached the limits of the prescribed advance.

While most of the PRCT had been involved with the 106th and 30th Infantry Division, the 2nd Battalion moved from Goronne to Neuville for assignment to the 7th Armored Division. Colonel Seitz and his men were assigned to Combat Command A at Polleux. On January 20, Task Force Seitz attacked south from an assembly area near Am Kreuz to capture Auf der Hardt woods and formed defensive positions on the southern edge. On reaching the objective, a patrol was sent to the village of Hochkreuz. At 1500, Company F was detailed to join a tank company for an attack on Born.

On January 22, the task force led CCA through In der Eidt Woods and closed in attack positions a mile north-west of Hunnange. At 1700, TOT concentrations were fired on Hunnange and the attack moved out. Time On Target (TOT) is the military co-ordination of artillery fire by many weapons so that all the munitions arrive at the target at roughly the same time. The US Army standard for coordinating a time-on-target strike is plus or minus three seconds from the prescribed time of impact.

By dark, Task Force Seitz had overrun Neider Emmels and Hunnange and was in contact with other 7th Armored Division forces.

Defensive positions were taken facing south and southwest. A roadblock was established at Lorentswaldchen, and patrols were sent to the outskirts of Saint Vith. At 1400 on January 23, Combat Command B passed through Task Force Seitz and completed the capture of Saint Vith.

On January 24 orders were given to clear the Saint Vith-Ambleve Road that remained in enemy hands. At 0600 on January 25, the battalion moved out for its attack position. By 1400, the objectives were secured.

On February 1 the 517th PRCT joined the 82nd near Honsfeld. The next day the 1st Battalion took up a blocking position to protect the northern flank of the 325th Glider Infantry while the 3rd Battalion moved into position to support, if required. All objectives of the attack plan were met, and on February 3, the PRCT received orders attaching it to the 78th Infantry Division at Simmerath.

THE SCHMIDT MINEFIELD

During the night of February 5, A and B Companies of the 517th attempted to cross the Kall River to secure a high observation point. To do this they were forced to move through minefields in view of the enemy. These fields were determined to have been the most extensively mined by the Germans that were encountered by the Allies during WWII. The 596th Parachute Combat Engineer Company was called forward to breach the minefield, while under intensive enemy small arms and automatic weapons fire. By their daring and valor, the engineers cleared a breach, enabling the infantry to pass through.

The 78th was to attack east on February 6 to seize Schmidt and the Schwammenauel Dam. The 517th PRCT was to move north to the Kleinhau-Bergstein area, relieve elements of the 8th Infantry and attack south from Bergstein during darkness on February 5 to seize the Schmidt-Nideggen Ridge.

The Germans had prepared the strongest defenses of the Western Front in this area.

By 0600 on the morning of February 5, all units had closed at Kleinhau. The German line ran from Zerkall west and South of Hill 400 to the Kall River. After dark the 2nd and 3rd Battalions moved into attack positions. Five to six hundred yards below Bergstein, both battalions hit minefields and concertina wire. The troopers attempted to move forward by crawling and probing, but all efforts proved futile. Men were blown up by Schu mines, Tellermines, and S-mines known as Bouncing Bettys. In Bergstein the troopers found some protection from small-arms fire but little else.

In mid-morning, the 596th Engineers began working in relays to clear a lane through the largest minefield encountered by the Allies in World War II while under direct enemy observation and fire. For thirty-six hours the 596th continued this genuinely heroic effort. In the 1st Battalion area, Company A sent a patrol from Hill 400 to Zerkall.

In the early afternoon of February 7, Colonel Graves was informed that the 517th was released from the 78th Division and attached to the 82nd Airborne in place. Task Force A had been formed, consisting of the 517th and the 505th Parachute Infantry. The 517th was to continue its planned attack.

During darkness on February 7, the 1st and 2nd Battalions prepared to go on the attack. At 2145, the 2nd Battalion moved down the lane through the minefields. By 0100, Company E and the remains of Company F were at the edge of the Kall Ravine. Forty-five minutes later, First Battalion was 400 yards southeast of Hill 400. North of the Kall, the 2nd Battalion troopers came under savage machine gun and mortar fire. The 1st Battalion rearranged to Hill 400. At noon a 3rd Battalion patrol was sent west to contact the 505th at the predesignated point on the Kall. Three efforts to reach the point were turned back by machine gun fire.

DISSOLUTION OF THE 517TH PARACHUTE REGIMENTAL COMBAT TEAM

The strength of the three 517th Battalions, now reduced to company size, were relieved by the 508th Parachute Infantry that night.

After being relieved, the PRCT was trucked to the railhead at Aachen, Germany. Two days later, the train arrived at Laon, France, where they settled in for another two-day stay. On February 15, Colonel Graves was notified by the XVIII Airborne Corps that the PRCT was assigned to the newly arrived 13th Airborne Division and was to proceed to Joigny, France, seventy miles southeast of Paris.

As the PRCT closed in at Joigny on February 21, news was received that the unit would be dissolved and merged with the 13th Airborne Division. Artillery and the engineers were merged with Company B, 129th Airborne Engineer Battalion.

On March 12, the 13th Airborne was assigned by the 1st Allied Airborne Army to participate in *Operation Varsity*, Montgomery's crossing of the Rhine River.

Shortly thereafter, decisions were made to call off the 13th's participation in the operation. It was the first of several aborted missions. Before its dissolution just shy of three years of service, the 517th Parachute Regimental Combat Team of 2,400 men endured heavy fighting in Italy (near Anzio), invaded southern France (Operation Dragoon), and literally walked through the bitter winter of the Ardennes (Battle of the Bulge), finally thrusting into Germany over the Rhine River through the Hurtgen Forest.

The war in Europe ended soon thereafter and the 13th Airborne Division was scheduled for shipment to the Pacific, where they were to participate in *Operation Cornet*, a jump into the Japanese home islands, with takeoff from the Alaskan Aleutian Islands.

During the unit's relatively brief lifetime, members of the 517th Regimental Parachute Combat Team earned 1 Medal of Honor, 6 Distinguished Service Crosses, 5 Legions of Merit, 131 Silver Stars, 631 Bronze Stars, 2 Air Medals, 4 Soldiers Medals, 17 French Croix De Guerre's, and 1,576 Purple Hearts—at a total cost of 252 killed in action.

Following formal deactivation of the team, seven veterans of the unit went on to attain the rank of general in the US Army, and one became sergeant major of the Army. Lieutenant Lippman went on to fight in Korea five years later, and in Vietnam twenty years later, while holding the line against oppressive armies. He was awarded a Distinguished Service Cross, Distinguished Service Medal, two Silver Stars and two Bronze Stars before the end of his military commitment.

Where does America get such gallant men?

Gordon's awards at the age of twenty, for bravery in the face of a determined and fanatical enemy, included a battlefield commission to second lieutenant, the Bronze Star, French Croix, Belgium Croix, and the Presidential Unit Citation.

BRONZE STAR

> For meritorious service in action against the enemy in the European Theater of Operations as a member of the First Battalion, 517th Parachute Infantry Regiment from May 1944 to February 1945. Lieutenant Lippman (then Staff Sergeant) on numerous occasions displayed outstanding courage and leadership in combat. Although he operated almost continuously without a platoon leader, his

judgment and initiative were highly commendable. Despite the loss of all but four of his original personnel during this period, he received and organized replacements and continued to perform with high combat efficiency, thereby playing a large part in the successful completion of all combat missions assigned to the Battalion.

CHAPTER 7

SIX-TWO-FIVE

The hard decisions are not the ones you make in the heat of battle. Far harder to make are those involved in speaking your mind about some harebrained scheme which proposes to commit troops to action under conditions where failure is almost certain, and the only results will be the needless sacrifice of priceless lives.

—GENERAL MATTHEW RIDGEWAY, US ARMY CHIEF OF STAFF

BOLD INITIATIVE

Gordon's mother, Arleen, was bold, having the ingenuity to help start up two local volunteer civic organizations in the early 1940s—not something a woman typically would do in those days. She also participated in many local civic events as a determined female in a male-dominated society.

She bought, and operated A&H Grocery in Hill City as a well-known and respected retail establishment for more than forty years. One of her endearing qualities was that she would give her neighbors credit on a smile and a handshake.

Gordon displayed these same traits of boldness, compassion, and empathy. It takes boldness to win the day. He walked in front of his team, and rallied them into battle from the front, not the rear. He didn't ask his men to do anything he wasn't willing to do himself. He took the first shot, tackled the first problem, discovered the first sign of trouble, distracted the enemy's attention away from his troopers. He knew that if he wanted any simple rewards like rest, food, and peace, he would have to be bold and seize the moment.

ALPHA MALE

In the years following victory in Europe, Gordon busied himself and finished high school, got married, started a family and built on his Army career.

He met his future bride in 1943 at a soda fountain shop where she worked. Gordon walked in one day, sat down at the counter, smiled, and ordered a drink, saying "I'd like a root beer float and hold the bubbles." That line worked, and they carried on a letter-writing campaign for the next three years while Gordon was on the East Coast, then in Europe fighting to save the world from Nazi fascism. Once the war was over, and as soon as he could get off on furlough, Gordon flew to Southern California and married his sweetheart, Lucille Meier, on July 1, 1946.

He received his high school diploma in 1947 from the Lemmon School District at the ripe old age of twenty-three.

As a young Army officer, he served in various capacities, as platoon leader and as an aide-de-camp to Major General Gavin, who was the 82nd Airborne commander in Fort Bragg. He excelled as a student in the Cavalry School at Fort Riley, became the Battalion Combat Team S2 (intelligence officer) in Pine Camp and aerial photo interpreter back with the 82nd Airborne again.

He was intent on making his career in the Army, becoming very familiar with Army protocols and language, and constantly seeking to increase his knowledge.

The 1947 photo and accompanying newspaper clipping below also display his mastery at jumping out of aircraft flying high or low, long before it became a competition sport of the Army Golden Knight Squadron.

From the newspaper account: ". . . Company of the Division marched up to a C-47 that stood directly in front of the grandstands holding over 12,000 people and loaded into it. After taking off a group of fighter planes made sweeps over the stands and then the C-47 made three passes at the field, dropping five men each time. A small liaison plane then flew by with Lt. Gordon J. Lippman, of Division G-2 Office, perched on one wing. As the little plane came over the field he jumped and unfurled a large American flag that he waved in the breeze while he floated down."

"It would be an embellishment to suggest this was the first experimental jump that eventually developed from low-level wing jumping to high-altitude jumping with oxygen," said Gordon's son, Mike, recently.

Mike added, "That bulky parachute was not maneuverable. I would have loved to see this landing without bending his knees or rolling, while hitting the ground and keeping the flag from touching it and managing a fully deployed chute in the process. Mind you, this was not what we know today as an acrobatic chute. He was a master parachutist indeed!"

Just to explain Mike's comments further, twelve years later, in 1959, nineteen Airborne Soldiers from various military units formed the Strategic Army Command Parachute Team (STRAC). Brigadier General Joseph Stilwell, Jr. gathered the soldiers with the intent of competing in the relatively new sport of skydiving, which at that time was dominated by the Soviet Union.

That year, the US Army team began representing the United States on the international competition circuit, and performed its first demonstration in Danville, Virginia. Two years later, the Department of Defense announced that the STRAC team would become the United States Army Parachute Team.

By 1962, the team earned the nickname the "Golden Knights." *Golden* signified the gold medals the team had won while *Knights* alluded to the team's ambition to conquer the skies. There is no doubt that if this team was formed while Gordon was younger, he would have tried out for a spot on the team.

An alpha male he was.

Promoted to first lieutenant on January 16, 1947, Gordon was not initially assigned to combat duty when the Korean War broke out. He continued to fulfill various duties as a platoon leader, assistant adjutant, company executive officer (XO) and battalion S2 officer with the 505th AIR (Airborne Infantry Regiment) in Fort Bragg, North Carolina.

But as the need arose in Korea for experienced combat officers after the outbreak of hostilities, he was called on to join the fight. The Army reassigned him in September 1950. As the North Korean Army pressed hard against the Allies, his first combat duty in Southeast Asia was to serve as a platoon leader for the 24th Infantry Regiment. He would join his new unit, which was already heavily engaged in combat, having suffered huge losses of officers.

The title of this chapter, Six-Two-Five, refers to the name given to this event by South Korea. It recognizes the date, June 25, 1950, when North Korea invaded the south. The Korean War is often regarded as the Forgotten War, as it lacked a lot of public attention. Though it lacked attention, there were a lot of military personnel and civilians killed or wounded due to the war. It's estimated that around 2.5 million civilians were either wounded, killed, missing, or abducted during the war, while over 2 million troops were either killed, wounded, or missing.

American military history records the feats of many famous commands, such as the "Big Red One" (1st Infantry Division), the 7th

Cavalry, and the 27th ("Wolfhound") Infantry Regiments. But accounts of the Korean War scarcely mention the 24th Infantry Regiment.

The unit had a distinguished history going back to the late nineteenth century horse soldier days in the Old West frontier. The 24th was involved in some of the fiercest fighting during the American Frontier Wars and gave a tremendous performance.

Yet it was disbanded in Korea and the men dispersed to fill battalions in other regiments. Some veterans of the command remain bitter over what they consider unnecessary and vindictive action on the US Army's part because of the unique nature of the unit.

The 24th Infantry Regiment was an all-Black unit, led by White officers, and Gordon was assigned to become one of those officers in the heat of a running gun battle. Gordon was introduced as Company A platoon leader, and became familiar with his men, and they learned about his character, while under some fierce enemy fire.

This chapter of Gordon's story weaves the fabric of 1950s Korea with this segregated Black regiment. The 24th was the single remaining Army regiment to fight in Korea as a segregated unit. The fact that these troops were commanded by White and Black officers in itself was unique.

Based on his leadership skills, history of performance in Italy, France, Belgium, and Germany under fire, Gordon was assigned as a platoon leader in this racially unstable scenario, and expected to rally the men, firm up their defenses, and hold the line.

The book *Black Soldier: White Army,* by the United States Army Center of Military History, is a powerful, unvarnished account of the experiences of the African American 24th Infantry Regiment, which was stigmatized for its deficiencies while its accomplishments passed largely into oblivion. In the end, many soldiers of the 24th Infantry Regiment were recognized for their courage and determination to win their battles.

Details about the history of the 24th and background leading up to 1950 tell the story of courageous men. Through interviews of the participants and riveting stories about their treatment, we learn how this segregated unit was thrust into the Korean War fully unprepared for combat.

The 24th was assigned to the 25th Infantry Division on February 1, 1946. By 1950, it was the only one of the twelve US Army infantry regiments in four divisions occupying post-WWII Japan that had all three of its authorized battalions, in part because all African American soldiers transferred to Japan were eventually sent to the 24th Infantry Regiment. The other eleven regiments had only two battalions each.

Black Soldier, White Army is an exhaustive report on the conditions surrounding the 24th Infantry Regiment during their time in Japan and Korea, before the US Army disbanded the unit. The following quote reflects the Regiment's plight: "In some ways, the 24th as a whole was better off than the all-White portions of the Eighth Army. In others, it was poorly prepared. In a few, because of its segregated nature, it was at a definite disadvantage."

On the positive side, the regiment was up to strength with a full complement of men, a characteristic of few other American units in Japan at the time. In addition, all of its battalions had passed their tests. Two had even participated in rudimentary regiment-level exercises at Gifu (Japan) with portions of their supporting engineering, artillery, and tank elements.

If the 24th was one with the rest of the Eighth Army in many of the difficulties it experienced, its segregated nature nonetheless compounded every problem.

Over the years, some of the White officers assigned to the unit had come to view themselves as outcasts. Their Black counterparts meanwhile had no doubt that the Army considered them second-class soldiers and that the military system they served was designed to prevent them from moving ahead.

The Black soldiers stayed on because life at Gifu and in the Army appeared a cut above what was available to them in the civilian world, and they clearly made every attempt on that account to keep up appearances. Beneath the surface, however, neither group associated much with the other, and mutual respect and trust were often in short supply.

The 24th was one of the original Buffalo Soldier units that was formed during the late nineteenth century on the western plains in the US. It received that title along with the 9th Cavalry and 25th Infantry Regiment from Native Americans, though the true reason for the nickname is unknown. The 24th was formed on November 1, 1869, in Fort McKavett Texas.

While in Korea, the 24th Infantry Regiment racked up an impressive record. Between 1950 and 1951, the unit earned 2 Medals of Honor (MOH), 23 Distinguished Service Crosses (DSC), 261 Silver Stars (SS), 537 Bronze Stars (BS) and 4,887 Purple Hearts (PH) all for bravery in the face of a daunting, fanatical, and determined enemy force.

WHY KOREA?

Although known as the Hermit Kingdom because of its isolation, Korea had still experienced occupying foreign troops many times in its history—most notably and recently with the Japanese occupation that started before WWII. In its ancient history it had been invaded by Chinese, Mongols, Manchus, and Japanese. The opening of its ports and permission of international trade in the late nineteenth century signaled to China, Japan, and Russia that Korea was up for grabs.

China considered Korea to be a buffer between itself and Japan.

The Japanese had eyed the peninsula for decades because it provided a strategic approach to Manchuria and China.

The Soviet Union, not to be outdone, wanted Korea as a convenient land bridge into Southeast Asia.

Since the late nineteenth century, Japan had ruled Korea, eventually turning it into a fiefdom and governing the peninsula to further its own interests.

With the end of World War II, the Soviets saw an opportunity on the long-sought-after peninsula. With the Japanese Empire defeated by the Allies, they quickly gained a foothold, easily and without a fight.

Once firmly in place, the Soviet Union effectively set up a puppet government, the North Korean People's Army (NKPA) and named Kim Il Sung as prime minister. Korea was occupied quickly and the anticipated freedom that should have come to the Korean people with the surrender of the Japanese, never materialized thanks to the Communist Soviet Union.

Between 1945 and the outbreak of hostilities in mid-1950, the northern and southern parts of Korea could not reconcile their political differences to become one nation. Nor was there any intent to establish two zones of occupation.

The Soviets maintained North Korea as a satellite state, creating a Communist constitution, stifling political dissent, and establishing a military, political, and economic enclave subservient to Moscow.

There never had been any agreement that Korea would be divided into two states, but in the vacuum created by the withdrawal of US forces from the south after WWII, and with the forcefulness of the Soviet regime's rejection of US proposals to the Joint Soviet-US Commission, the 38th Parallel became the de facto division of the country. The fact is, both parts of Korea were unofficially considered to be protectorates of their respective occupying powers.

There is little doubt that the Soviets conceived and swiftly executed a plan that encompassed their goals of expansion in the Far East. Their timetable included declaration of war on Japan at the end of WWII, a forceful entry into North Korea to set up a Communist government, and repeated inflexibility in resolving the issue of a united Korea. This all proceeded on schedule and it appeared there was little the Western powers could do to delay or stop the ultimate division.

After all, the West had remained at a safe distance while the Soviet Union swiftly moved into Eastern Europe to establish satellite Communist states closing out WWII. The United States was not prepared to get into a fight with the Soviet Union so soon after World War II, and the Soviets were masters in the art of subverting or controlling people that had just gone through—or were in the midst of—socioeconomic or political crises.

The inability of the two powers to reach an agreement on the independence of all Korea did not bode well for the future of the country. Finally, despairing of success in the face of the Soviet position, the United States set the issue before the United Nations in 1947, which quickly called for national elections open to both North and South Koreans in the following year.

The Soviets refused to honor the free elections in the north. In the south, however, a national assembly was elected, a democratic constitution was drawn, a president elected, and the Republic of Korea was formally and legally established. The Soviets refused to accept the Republic of Korea as the legally constituted and valid government in Korea. Not surprisingly, when the issue was presented to the United Nations, the Soviets vetoed membership of the Republic of Korea.

While the Soviets had ostensibly withdrawn the bulk of their armed forces from Korea in late 1948, there remained a cadre of advisers of every sort—political, economic, and military—who were determined to make the country into a puppet state.

At the same time, the withdrawal of US occupation troops from southern Korea commenced, and by June 1949 only a small group of American advisers remained behind to train Korean security forces. The Soviets concluded that the United States no longer wished to maintain a military presence in Korea, placing the country up for grabs again.

On June 25, 1950, with the blessing of the Soviets, the North Korean People's Army (NKPA) launched a full-scale invasion across the 38th Parallel against the South Korean Republic of Korea (ROK). The North Korean attack found the remaining US forces totally inadequate.

As a nation, America was dismally unprepared for another war so soon or so far away. When President Truman responded with a request that United Nations members oppose North Korea's aggression, in order to restore peace in Korea, America had few fighting divisions. Those that were closest to the action were all undermanned, partially equipped, and for the most part, made up of men who had not seen combat action in WWII.

America was not politically, economically, psychologically, or militarily prepared to conduct war in the summer of 1950. North Korea took advantage of those conditions and rolled into the south almost unopposed.

Nevertheless, the immediate action undertaken by the United States was to dispatch a task force of the 25th Infantry Division by air to Korea on July 2, 1950. This infantry engaged North Korean combat forces three days later, on July 5.

With this backdrop, the US Army literally was thrown into an armed conflict without sufficient planning, manpower, experience, skill, or equipment to push back the North Korean aggressors.

Upon landing at Pusan in the southern part of the peninsula, the 25th Infantry Division, to which the 24th Infantry Regiment was assigned, initially positioned itself 100 miles north and was assigned the mission of blocking and delaying advancing North Korean forces in the Naktong River valley from the northwest.

By July 21, the 3rd Battalion of the 24th, supported by other elements of the 24th Regimental Combat Team, conducted the first major offensive mission with its recapture of the vital crossroads town of Yechon, while driving out North Korean troops and repulsing all attempts by the NKPA to retake the town. It was considered by Congress and the Department of Defense as the first sizeable American ground victory—a little more than two weeks into the war.

The 25th Infantry Division remained in the upper Naktong River valley through August, near the town of Sangju. The regiments of the 25th conducted delaying actions, trading space for time against ever-increasing North Korean manpower and pressure.

Fearing a North Korean breakthrough to Pusan along the coast, the

25th Infantry Division was transferred more than 100 miles by trains and trucks. On August 1–3, 1950, they were stationed in the vicinity of Masan, a city situated astride the southern coast road approach from Pusan in the west. By August 3, the 25th Division was in its new defensive positions extending twenty miles in width, from the southern coast north to the confluence of the Naktong and Nam rivers.

The 24th Infantry Regiment held the center of this line in the rugged mountain ridges and peaks of Subok-san to include Pil-bong and what came to be known as Battle Mountain. These mountain peaks had no roads or trails leading up their eastern slopes, making it extremely difficult for US forces to attack vertically.

This resulted in the Army taking hours to resupply fighting units and bring down casualties. Strong, invasive NKPA attacks with overwhelming force hit the 25th line repeatedly. In the 24th Regiment sector, Battle Mountain and Pil-bong often were overrun and then retaken in hand-to-hand combat, resulting in heavy casualties.

On August 6, elements of the 3rd Battalion near the village of Haman were ambushed by NKPA troops. Pfc. William Thompson, Company M, 24th Infantry, took up a machine gun in an exposed position and placed accurate fire on the attacking North Koreans until being mortally wounded. Sacrificing himself, he gave his unit time to react to the attack, for which he was posthumously awarded the Medal of Honor for unselfish heroism.

Through August and into September, the 25th Division successfully held its defensive sector, preventing North Korean forces from breaking through to Pusan. For this significant achievement, the division, along with the 24th Infantry, was awarded a Republic of Korea Presidential Unit Citation.

Operating in defense of Masan, the 25th Division placed its 24th Infantry and 5th Infantry Regiments on Sobuk-san to defend its two peaks, P'il-bong and Hill 665, which later would become known as Battle Mountain. This action involved the struggle between United Nations Command (UN) and North Korean forces early in the war, from August 15 to September 19, 1950. It was one of several large engagements fought simultaneously during the Battle of Pusan Perimeter.

The battle ended in a victory for the UN after large numbers of United States Army (US) and Republic of Korea Army (ROK) troops were able to prevent a North Korean People's Army (NKPA) division from capturing the mountain area.

What followed was a month-long struggle with the NKPA 6th Division, in which Battle Mountain changed hands twenty times.

During the deadlock, neither side was able to secure a definitive victory in capturing the mountaintop, but the US forces succeeded in their mission of preventing the NKPA from advancing beyond Battle Mountain, paving the way for the NKPA's eventual defeat and withdrawal.

Later, and in conjunction with General MacArthur's surprise landing of X Corps at Inchon on September 15, 1950, the United Nations forces in the Pusan Perimeter went on the offensive.

In the 25th Division sector, strong enemy resistance on the mountain peaks of Subok-san delayed undertaking the offensive until September 19, when the mountain peaks and ridges had been cleared by the 24th Infantry Regiment in the face of weakening but stubborn enemy resistance.

The cost of these battles became quite high, with officers and enlisted men falling to incapacitating combat wounds, resulting in death for some.

Gordon Lippman arrived in early September to assume his role as an Able Company platoon leader in the face of this horror, replacing his predecessor in the 24th Infantry Regiment in the midst of this skirmish.

CHAPTER 8

BATTLE MOUNTAIN

ONCE THE MOUNTAINS WERE IN friendly hands, the 25th Division went on the offensive again. An attack to the west on two lines of advance was to be conducted with motorized task forces, which consisted primarily of the 24th Infantry Regiment.

Starting on September 27, and moving rapidly, that task force brushed aside North Korean delaying actions, rapidly seizing several Korean towns, and in the process managed to liberate close to 100 American prisoners of war. By September 30, the 24th Infantry had reached and liberated the west coast port city of Kunsan.

On October 29, 1950, almost two months after he was assigned to the 24th, Gordon was elevated to Able Company commanding officer (CO).

Able Company was temporarily assigned the role of acting military governor of the city of Kunsan, which meant that Able effectively controlled the activities of the civilian population in that area. First Lieutenant Lyle Rishell had been promoted to company executive officer (XO) under Lt. Lippman.

In Rishell's book *With a Black Platoon in Combat*, written more than a decade later, Rishell says of Gordon: "He was a fine officer, a strong leader, and we got along great right from the outset. I admired him tremendously, and the days I served under him were some of the best of my career. He was a hard, no-nonsense officer, but he was fair and an inspiration for all of us in that place."

In October, after linking up with X Corps, the Eighth Army had crossed the 38th Parallel into North Korea while the 25th Infantry Division remained in South Korea. The 24th Infantry Regiment and other elements of the 25th Division were given the mission of eliminating surviving fragments of North Korean units south and east of the city of Taejon. These stragglers had been bypassed by American forces and were threatening the American supply lines.

By early November, the 25th Division had successfully accomplished its mission of securing and stabilizing the area around Taejon and was moved north to Kaesong to continue the mission of eliminating pockets of bypassed enemy units along the 38th Parallel.

Rishell goes on to detail their next move:

> We awoke with the sound of rain beating against the broken windows. What a hellish day for a move! The poor weather did not generate much enthusiasm, but we crawled from our mountain bags, pulled on our dirty clothes and boots, and went over to the mess tent for breakfast. We gulped down a breakfast of scrambled eggs, bacon, bread, jam, and coffee.
>
> While we ate, Lt. Lippman went over the day's details. The compound, which normally was hard and dry, had become a quagmire of gluey, soft clay. It caked on the boots to form lead weights, a miserable mess. Our orders were to move on the arrival of transportation, but the only vehicles coming available were three quarter-ton trucks. We were still on the Main Supply Route (MSR), which meant that two platoons still on guard duty had to remain

behind until transport could be arranged for them to follow. The 24th had been assigned to protect that route but new orders meant they would give up that protection detail.

The rest of us packed our gear, rolled up blankets and sleeping bags, and waited for transportation to the trains. On arrival at So-Jongni after dark, we spent the night in bivouac and then most of the next day waiting for transport to our next stop. We then loaded onto rail cars for the train ride up north.

These were very unwelcoming box cars which we squeezed in to. It became apparent there was no plan to send us into reserve or back to Japan, which caused a solemn uneasiness to come over the men. The NCOs oriented their men in preparation for fighting as soon as we would dismount.

The loading and waiting had not done much for the men's morale, but fortunately the day warmed a bit, and we began to get more comfortable. Along the way we saw hordes of refugees carry everything they owned on their backs, climbing on board the flat cars. The train moved on, and went through Suwon and then Seoul after dark. By daybreak, we reached Ilsan, north of Seoul near the 38th Parallel.

Task Force Lippman, composed of Company A with attachments from the intelligence and reconnaissance (I and R) platoon, one section each of heavy mortars, 81mm mortars, machine guns, and 75mm recoilless rifles, was to proceed to the town of Yonchon above the 38th Parallel and secure the town against any invaders attempting to seize it.

The composition of Task Force Lippman and order of march into what became known as the Iron Triangle was 1st Platoon in the lead

with the 3rd Platoon, ROK Platoon, and 2nd Platoon following. The
Command Group teams would follow fourth. The 4.2mm, 81mm
mortar teams would bring up the rear. At 0530, the task force was
to enter the town. At 0545, all unit commands checked radios. As
soon as possible they were to notify Lieutenant Costello by message
when the town was reasonably secure.

Many firefights ensued, lives were lost, and trucks destroyed in
an enemy ambush. The fighting was only getting more intense and
Japan became a distant memory.

Company A had launched a coordinated attack on Yonchon
with elements of the 17th ROK Regiment and 800 South Korean
policemen. Striking in the early morning after a preliminary thirty-
minute mortar barrage, this UN force captured the town in less than
three hours. Thirteen North Korean soldiers were captured. Later
in the day the I and R Platoon was ambushed. The enemy knocked
out the lead and rear vehicles of the convoy and set several on fire.

Members of the American patrol leapt from their vehicles to
defend themselves, the Reds charged and inflicted heavy casualties.
It was not the first ambush to hit division troops, and it would not
be the last. North Koreans continued to use this form of attack
frequently in the days ahead, and UN forces took heavy casualties
as they continued on with their mission.

The Americans were north of the 38th Parallel, moving deep into
enemy territory on November 19 near Anju. Taking the offensive,
the 25th Division quickly ran into stiff resistance and was thrown
onto the defensive as massive Chinese Communist forces attacked
and penetrated the 8th Army right flank. This opened up the 25th
Division's right, which was held by the 24th Infantry Regiment.
Taking heavy casualties as the Chinese hit the right flank of the 2nd
Battalion, and with Chinese troops moving to their rear, the 24th
Infantry, along with the rest of the 25th Division, began a series of
delaying actions while backpedaling down the peninsula.

Of the many men throughout the 25th Infantry Division to

distinguish themselves in these battles, Lt. Lippman is only one. The commendation below outlines his heroic actions in November:

SILVER STAR MEDAL CITATION

The President of the United States of America, authorized by Act of Congress July 9, 1918, takes pleasure in presenting the Silver Star to First Lieutenant (Infantry) Gordon Joseph Lippman, United States Army, for gallantry in action as a member of Company A, 1st Battalion, 24th Infantry Regiment, 25th Infantry Division. During the early morning hours of 27 November 1950 near Ipsok, Korea, a strong hostile force attacked the supply train of Lieutenant Lippman's battalion. Despite exposure to intense hostile fire, he organized the supply troops in a perimeter defense and led the machine gun crew to vantage points from which they could direct effective counterfire on the attacking enemy. Advancing through a deadly small arms and mortar barrage, he contacted the supply area of an adjacent unit, thus enabling the two forces to combine their strength and repel the hostile incursion. Lieutenant Lippman's valorous actions are in keeping with the high traditions of the United States Armed Forces.

The unit reached Kaesong on December 8 and then moved south of the Imjin River by December 14. Continuing Chinese pressure forced the 8th Army to withdraw further south to the 37th Parallel near Osan by January 3, 1951.

When he finally found time, Gordon wrote a letter to Lucille on December 11, 1950. It read:

The last time I wrote to you was on Thanksgiving Day. The next day we pushed off and moved steady for three days over hill and dale. The night of the third day we stopped moving in a northerly direction and began a southerly move. That was a night I'll never forget, all the lights on the pinball machine lit up, old Joe began blowing bugles and whistles and hollering bingo and the jig was up. Old Dad has played mountain goat a few times before but this one took the cake. I felt like one of those greyhound dogs chasing a cotton rabbit, legs straight out and belly on the ground. We moved day and night for I don't know how long covering about 250 map miles, which is about 500 walking miles in this country up and down. We had about two or three meals the first six days and after that things picked up a little. We would throw ears of corn in an open fire and char them black and devour them. I didn't ever know I loved charred corn so much until then. Once in a while my Korean boy found some beans or potatoes or rice so we kept from starving. I didn't mind the hungry feeling so much cause the damned Chinese laundry men kept running as fast as I did (but they didn't get to press my clothes) until they got tired and then I still kept running awhile to put a little breathing distance between us. Sure feels funny to be the chased instead of the chaser.

PS. I've got a valet now. He carries my pack and digs my holes. This is quite a war. The only English he can speak is his name, "Hogan."

PPS. One of the company officers shot a pheasant this morning so we had a fine dinner. Hogan roasted it over an open fire. I've gained about five pounds.

On January 25, the 25th Division participated in a United Nations counteroffensive, reaching the Han River twenty-five days later. On March 7, the 24th Infantry conducted a well-executed assault crossing of the Han as other elements of the 25th Division drove north to inflict heavy casualties on Communist forces.

Since Gordon had been involved in active ground combat operations for another 180 days, a star designating his 2nd Combat Infantry Badge award was issued by the US Army on March 21, 1951. Gordon, however, was focused on his ground mission with the Chinese and North Korean Armies putting up a determined fight to slow him down.

The unit reached and held a line just south of the city of Chorwon by the end of March. After crossing the Hantan River on April 11, the 1st Battalion, 24th Infantry attacked a steep ridgeline defended by heavily dug-in Chinese forces at about 0430. The Americans took the initiative to attack without the normal preparatory artillery barrage that would have signaled imminent assault. By using this approach, the 24th surprised the Chinese and found them very disorganized but the entrenched enemy was able to repulse the attack.

At the higher levels of command and control during this period, a dramatic change in leadership took place. On this same day, half a world away in Washington DC, following a series of public utterances that revealed sharp differences over national policy and military strategy, President Truman took a bold step by relieving General Douglas MacArthur of all his commands. Replacing him with General Ridgway and dispatching Lieutenant General James A. Van Fleet posthaste to take command of the 8th Army and attached forces. Van Fleet arrived and assumed command three days later on April 14. With the opinionated and defiant MacArthur out of the way, President Truman was free to pursue a less aggressive military strategy that resulted in the stalemate we see now almost seventy years later. Once again, political expediency triumphed over military strategy, resulting in greater loss of life and less-than-ideal results.

Back on the ground in Korea in early April 1951, soldiers carrying out their orders had to creatively overcome some of their own obstacles.

Problems in the 1st Battalion's zone began almost as soon as they set out on their mission. The patrol that had surveyed the crossing at the Hantan River had apparently made its measurements by eye rather than by tape. When the engineers arrived days later with precut timbers, they found that the gap they had to span was at least fifteen feet longer than expected.

Because of the delay in construction that followed, Able and Bravo Companies had no choice but to wade across the river. As they did, several of the men slipped and were swept away, causing enough of a commotion to alert the enemy.

As a result, when the first platoon to enter the river reached the far shore and proceeded up the bank, it was met with a challenge shouted in the Chinese language followed by a hail of grenades and machine-gun fire.

Outlined in the citation below, Gordon earned his second Silver Star in this skirmish at Do Chung on April 11, 1951. Eye-witness accounts were considered in the award evaluation process. Noted on the July 7, 1951 recommendation for his subsequent Distinguished Service Cross (DSC), written almost three months after the battlefield action, was that Gordon had previously earned two Purple Hearts, a Silver Star, and two Bronze Stars.

SILVER STAR COMMENDATION:

> The enemy was on high ground defending a river crossing site . . . Comrades of individual were pinned down by fire and for the most part were unable to assist in act. On the morning of 11 April 1951, Company A, 24th Infantry Regiment was to affect a river crossing of the Hantan River, in the vicinity of Do Chung, Korea, during the hours of darkness.

Mission was to seize high ground overlooking crossing site. Lieutenant Lippman, commanding Company A, realizing that the success of the battalion operation depended upon Company A completing its mission, left his command position and went to the head of his company to personally lead them across the river. Just before the crossing was completed an enemy outpost discovered the operation and brought machine gun fire upon the helpless soldiers who were caught in the middle of the river. Lieutenant Lippman immediately took his lead squad and moved on the enemy position, he deployed his men and in a fast-determined assault into the face of the heavy enemy fire and destroyed the enemy position, thus allowing his company to continue crossing with a minimum of casualties. Upon completion of the crossing, Lieutenant Lippman reorganized his company and deployed them for an attack on the high ground representing their final objective. To reach this high ground it was necessary to cross about 300 yards of flat ground which offered no cover or concealment. As the company started across this flat ground they were brought under extremely heavy enemy small arms and automatic weapons fire. Lieutenant Lippman, still with the lead elements of the company, rallied his men and led the charge across the area. He reached the base of his objective with approximately one platoon; the remainder of the company being pinned down by the enemy fire. The objective was a steep hill defended by approximately one platoon of CCF (Chinese Communist Forces), well dug-in in a perimeter of fox holes around the top. Objective was approachable only by several narrow fingers. Lieutenant Lippman sized up the situation immediately and organized his men into small groups, sending each group up one of the narrow fingers. Realizing that these approaches were well covered by enemy fire and that the success of his attack depended upon the diversion of enemy fire from his attacking forces, Lieutenant Lippman, armed with a .45 automatic and several grenades charged up the slope to a position within six feet of one enemy foxhole and ten feet of another. Lieutenant Lippman was wounded early in the fray but continued to stand upright, firing his automatic and throwing hand grenades while his assault teams maneuvered up the narrow approaches. He was successful in diverting the enemy fire and after about forty-five minutes of remaining in his exposed position, his assault teams were able to close with the enemy, killing nine, capturing two, and putting the remainder to flight. Lieutenant Lippman, though wounded, refused to be evacuated until the position was consolidated and company was firmly entrenched for defense of position.

The act was outstanding in view of the cool courage displayed by Lieutenant Lippman, was more than normally expected in that he purposely drew the enemy fire in order to save casualties among his men. As a result of the act, Company A secured high ground overlooking the river crossing thereby allowing the battalion to cross and continue the assault on the enemy.

What follows are eye-witness accounts resulting in the awarding of this, his second Silver Star, describing his valorous actions in this fight.

Cpl. Asia J. Peterson, Headquarters Company, 1st Battalion, 24th Infantry Regiment, observed Lippman in his calculated assault on the enemy position.

> On 11 April 1951, I was runner for the Company Commander, Company A 24th Infantry Regiment, Lieutenant Lippman. We were the lead company in crossing the Hantan River and Lieutenant Lippman went to the front of the Company to lead them across.
>
> As we were crossing, a machine gun opened up on us and immediately Lieutenant Lippman took a squad of men and charged the enemy position, destroying the machine gun emplacement. We then maneuvered toward our objective, and while crossing about 300 yards of flat ground, we were hit by very heavy enemy small arms and automatic weapons fire.
>
> Lieutenant Lippman called to his company and led them on a dash into the fire at the base of the hill. He then split us into small assault teams and pointed out the route for us to take in assaulting the hill. Lieutenant Lipman then went up the hill to a spot within six feet of the enemy positions where he fired his automatic and threw his grenades into the enemy foxholes. In doing so he drew all the attention from the enemy and so we were able to advance up the hill without being fired on. When we closed with the enemy, Lieutenant Lippman, though wounded, would not leave the field until our company was dug in for defense.

MSgt. Willie N. Robinson, Company A, 24th Infantry Regiment also wrote down his observation:

On 11 April 1951, I was Platoon Sgt of the 2nd Platoon, Company A, 24th Infantry Regiment. My platoon was the lead platoon in river crossing of Hantan River. Lieutenant Lippman, the Company Commander, joined my platoon and personally led us across the river . . . When he had thrown all of his grenades, he threw his rations at the enemy.

The enemy soldiers concentrated their fire on Lieutenant Lippman thus making it easy for us to go up the approaches and engage the enemy in close combat. Lieutenant Lippman although wounded would not be evacuated until the position was organized.

Continuing to lead his men on their many perilous missions through a hail of gunfire and slopping through the rain and mud, Gordon rose to the challenge with one brilliant, decisive action after another. His Silver Star was subsequently upgraded to the Army's second highest award, the Distinguished Service Cross (DSC).

DISTINGUISHED SERVICE CROSS CITATION

The President of the United States of America, under the provisions of the Act of Congress approved July 9, 1918, takes pleasure in presenting the Distinguished Service Cross to Lieutenant (Infantry) Gordon J. Lippman, United States Army, for extraordinary heroism in connection with military operations against an armed enemy of the United Nations while serving as commanding officer of Company A, 1st Battalion, 24th Infantry Regiment, 25th Infantry Division.

Lieutenant Lippman distinguished himself by astonishing heroism in action against enemy aggressor forces in the vicinity of Do Chung, Korea, on 11 April

1951. On the morning of 11 April under cover of darkness Lieutenant Lippman moved to the head of his company in an assault crossing the Hantan River to secure the high ground across the river. An enemy outpost opened up on the company with intense automatic weapons fire, as they reached the middle of the river. Quickly deploying the lead squad, he moved among the men in an exposed position directing their fire and knocking out the enemy gunners, allowing his company to complete the river crossing with minimal casualties. He reorganized the company and and deployed the men for the attack on the enemy objective. As the company moved across flat exposed terrain they were again subjected to intense small arms and automatic weapons fire. Lieutenant Lippman moved among the men encouraging them and leading them across the area, reaching the bottom of the steep hill with approximately a platoon. The only approachable route was up several narrow ridges which were defended by an enemy platoon in well dug in positions forming a strong perimeter defense on the crest of the hill. After sending his men out in small groups toward the objective, he realized success depended on diverting the enemy's attention. He charged the enemy armed with a .45 Cal. Automatic and several hand grenades. For forty-five minutes he maneuvered to within a few yards of these positions, harassing the hostile troops and drawing their concentrated fire before reaching to within six feet of one enemy foxhole and ten feet away from another. Killing the occupants enabled his assault teams to close with the enemy and secure their objective. Although wounded early in this action, he refused to be evacuated until the position was consolidated and his company was firmly entrenched for defense of the position. The extraordinary heroism and outstanding leadership of Lieutenant Lippman was a source of pride and inspiration to his men and reflected utmost credit on himself and the military service.

This courageous action enabled the platoon to work its way to a position from which an assault was launched that routed the enemy.

With another reference to Gordon's actions above, we see Able Company taking the lead but coming under heavy fire and was immediately pinned down. That discouraged Charley Company from crossing the river, but strong leadership quickly asserted itself.

The commander of Able Company, who had crossed before his men, went back and rallied his troopers. By then, the engineers had repaired the bridge, so dodging machine-gun fire that continued to rake the structure, the men crossed and began their assault.

The knoll that commanded the area and the machine guns that had tormented them became their first objectives, with the company's 1st Platoon taking responsibility. The attackers were driven back several times by grenades and automatic weapons, but they kept trying, and after three attempts at about 0715, they captured the position.

The fighting was vicious. By 1835 on April 11, the men of the battalion were, as the unit's commander, Major Baranowski, reported, "pretty well beat up." Even so, the unit itself was well positioned in a crescent of companies along the south and southeastern approaches to the mountain.

Although enemy dugouts were present and might have provided convenient overnight protection for the men, most of the troopers, despite their fatigue, preferred to dig their own foxholes. The enemy's positions were full of dead bodies and infested with fleas.

Through the intense fighting and artillery shelling, some of the companies fell into disarray, alarming the 25th Division CO, Major General Joseph S. Bradley.

Bradley soon arrived at the 24th Infantry's command post to see for himself. Ten minutes after that, furious at the dissembling of the regiment's officers, he notified his command post that "3rd Battalion, 24th Infantry is disorganized and south of the river. I have directed Colonel Britt to reform the battalion on I Company, which had not crossed river.

"I have also directed that the battalion recross the river prior to dark, if that can be done in an organized fashion. If this cannot be done, the battalion will cross at daylight tomorrow."

In a comment that could only have sent chills through officers within earshot, Bradley ended his transmission by ordering his division's operations section to "make this conversation a matter of record."

This did not go well for Colonel Britt.

Two days later, through bitter fighting, on April 13, the ridge was taken by the 24th Infantry. The 1st Battalion secured Hill 642 by 1055, but at a cost of many casualties. The unit then began dispatching patrols to the northeast to protect the left flank of the 2nd Battalion, which was moving up to its right. Company A was down to about half strength and had only one officer remaining, a second lieutenant, which was, undeniably, a very high cost. That is why it was called Battle Mountain.

Due to his injuries sustained under heavy gunfire during the assault, Gordon had been removed from the line and reassigned as the assistant battalion S3 officer on April 17, 1951, while he recovered.

On April 22, the Chinese started a new offensive that pushed back the United Nations forces, including the 25th Division, to the area just north of Seoul.

Hard fought gains were given up under another enemy counteroffensive, but UN forces countered on May 20, driving the Chinese back north across the 38th Parallel.

Just over three weeks later and after recovering from his wounds, Gordon was elevated to battalion S3, a position he held until June 2, 1951, when he was moved to battalion S2 officer, taking responsibility for all battalion intelligence operations and security.

By the middle of June, the 25th Division had captured the town of Kumhwa and then, on June 21, they were taken off the line and placed in reserve near Uijongbu for some much-needed rest, relaxation, and refitting.

During this brief rest from battle, on June 27, 1951, Gordon was officially promoted to captain.

Armistice negotiations started on July 10, and in mid-July, the 25th went back on the line to its previous positions near the towns of Chorwon and Kumhwa.

Temporarily moving back to battalion S3 on July 24, Gordon would soon return to the line where combat leadership was sorely needed. But this time, he was assigned to the 34th Infantry Regiment just prior to the dissolution of the 24th Infantry Regiment.

While the armistice negotiations were underway, the two sides went on the defensive. One of the last significant combat actions of the 24th Infantry Regiment in Korea involved the regiment's Company F, which on September 15, 1951, captured a key Communist outpost with a gallant bayonet and grenade charge near the village of Mando.

Gordon finished out his tour in Korea as a company commanding officer in the 34th Infantry Regiment.

Shortly thereafter, and in conjunction with the US Army end of segregation, the 24th Infantry Regiment was inactivated, effective October 1, 1951, at Chipo-ri, Korea after six Korean War campaigns and eighty-two years of continuous service in the United States Army. The 24th Infantry Regiment was the last of the original four Buffalo Soldier units to see combat.

His unit, the 24th Infantry Regiment, earned 2 combat streamers for having 65% or more of their men earn the EIB (Expert Infantrymen Streamer) and the CIB (Combat Infantrymen Badge Streamer). Also, the 24th Infantry Regiment won two Republic of Korea Presidential Unit Citations (First on Aug 1-11 1950 at Chinju and the second 2000-2003 for the defense of Korea from the Korean Government celebrating their 50th anniversary of the Korean War). This last one was given to all personnel and units who served in that conflict.

On December 27, 1951, Captain Lippman was reassigned stateside as an instructor of tactics at the infantry school in Fort Benning, Georgia. His combat experiences and calm demeanor made him a valuable and knowledgeable teacher. This was a position he held for the next nine months, training and preparing soldiers. Fort Benning is the center of gravity in the Army for producing trained combat soldiers and is the primary driver for development of the future force.

Back in Korea, although the two sides agreed to an armistice in 1952, the Korean stand-off continues to this day as both sides square off at the 38th Parallel, where it all began.

CHAPTER 9

WHERE DOES AMERICA GET SUCH GALLANT MEN?

Military threats to peace can take many forms. Consequently, if our power is to serve its purpose, it must have characteristics which give it the capability of successfully countering the various forms of danger which are likely to occur: it must be broad in applicability and balanced in content.

—GENERAL MAXWELL D. TAYLOR, ARMY CHIEF OF STAFF

COMPASSION

He was kind, partly because paternal grandmother Edith taught him that kindness wasn't a weakness. He displayed a certain type of strength to be able to tell hard truths. He was kind enough and considerate enough to lay it all on the line. In combat, he was insightful enough to tell it like it is and not ramble into delusions of grandeur. He cared for the troopers under his command, and made sure they were well-supplied, well-fed, well-trained, and well-equipped.

MARRIAGE, FAMILY, AND EDUCATION

During an extensive tour of duty in Germany following Gordon's return from the Korean War, and unable to have children on their own, the young couple adopted three children, Mark, Mike, and Lura Lee. Their memories of life with their adoptive parents are recounted at the end of this book.

As a member of the Legion of Valor, Gordon was a rising star in the US Army, a devoted husband, and loving father. He began settling into family life in Virginia as the Army continued to assign him to increasing roles of accountability. Gordon then was sent to the National War College by his commander.

He was selected as one of the Army's future strategic leaders to learn high-level policy, command, and staff responsibilities through senior-level courses of study in national security strategy. Joining select ranking representatives from the Army, Air Force, Navy, Marine Corps, Coast Guard, Department of State, other federal agencies, and international fellows from foreign countries, Gordon studied joint and interagency strategies and tactics, learning advanced concepts of leadership at the international level.

He also attended the Army Staff College to learn about operational tactics, planning, and strategies with joint, multinational and interagency operations. These included teamwork, attitudinal behaviors and perspectives on cross-functional goals and objectives.

As a captain during his time with the 8th Infantry Division, Gordon wrote an article called, "Have the Confidence to Confide, which appeared in the August 1957 issue of *The Military Review*. It's a fascinating analysis of the leadership styles and failures of two famous Civil War Generals—one highly dysfunctional and the other highly respected.

Generals George Armstrong Custer and Stonewall Thomas J. Jackson fought on opposite sides of the war and held vastly differing concepts of leadership while displaying a lack of trust in their direct reports. A modified summation of his report follows:

While a single leader seldom is able to achieve complete mastery of the principles of leadership in their entirety, almost without exception great leaders consciously or unconsciously practice a majority of these principles.

These principles of leadership are in some cases so closely allied in meaning that at times it is hard to distinguish one from another. In violating principles such as *set the example* and *ensure that the task is understood, supervised, and accomplished,* General Custer also appears to have ignored the following: *keep your men informed, know your men, look out for their welfare,* and *make sound and timely decisions.* Frequently Custer showed a distinct failure to know himself and seek self-improvement.

While Stonewall Jackson was steadfast in the application of most of the principles of leadership, it was his violation of the principle of *ensure that the task is understood, supervised and accomplished* that cost the South heavily at the battle of Seven Days and later at Chancellorsville. Both times victory was within the grasp of General Robert E. Lee, and each time the loss of complete victory could be traced to Jackson who, like Custer, failed to *keep their men informed.*

Thus, it was that one man was a great leader in almost every aspect of that art, yet his downfall due to the fact that he could not or would not trust his subordinates was just as costly as that suffered by Custer, who violated almost every one of the sound principles of leadership.

Gordon, time and time again during his exceptional Army career, from Camp Toccoa through WWII, Korea, and Vietnam, proved that he not only understood these leadership principles but practiced what he preached about them and those around him noticed.

Gordon was a devout Roman Catholic, attending church in Vienna, Virginia, where Mark, Lura Lee, and Mike were all confirmed. "We always got donuts afterwards!" observed Mark. They attended Catholic Church in Council Grove, Kansas, while Gordon was stationed at Fort Riley.

Mark and Mike were Knights of the Altar in Council Grove, as well as in the post church at Carlisle Barracks after they moved back east. During grade school and even a bit during High School, they continued in their Knights of the Altar roles.

It was this spiritual ethos that propelled Gordon to maintain positive relationships and endeared him to his family, friends, superiors, peers, and subordinates alike. Disciplined in his personal life, principled in his professional life.

After receiving his next promotion, on June 17, 1958, to the rank of major, Gordon was sent to the National War College where he studied and wrote about Antoine Henri Jomini. An eighteenth-century professional soldier, Jomini served for more than sixty-nine years, at different times, on Napoleon's general staff, with the Swiss Army, and under Czar Alexander of Russia. The article was titled "The Theory and Nature of War," and it appeared in the 1959 Volume II edition of *The Command and Staff College* periodical, which was published by the Marine Corps Institute.

He clearly admired Jomini as both a historian and a tactician. This article contained an afterword by General Maxwell Taylor (see the opening of this chapter), who was then Army Chief of Staff under President Eisenhower.

He held other positions as an instructor at the US Army Infantry School, an advisor with the Army Reserve Advisory Group, and commander of the 8th Administrative Services Company, 8th US Infantry Division. He was a graduate of the 1955-56 Regular Course of the US Army Command and General Staff College, and served in the office of the chief of staff, 8th US Infantry Division.

In addition to his military studies, Gordon also was a student at the Department of State Foreign Service Institute, earned his Bachelor's degree in Business Administration from the University of Omaha in 1962, and a Master's Degree in International Affairs from Georgetown University in 1965. The high school dropout became an accomplished war hero and perennial student, proving that personal initiative and hard work will pay dividends.

In 1963, Gordon was recognized for his leadership, loyalty, and service with an appointment to the rank of lieutenant colonel. He had served the United States of America and the US Army for more than two decades teaching, leading, training, and mentoring younger, and sometimes, older soldiers. He held countless intelligence, logistics, operational, public relations, administrative, and combat roles.

With a highly regarded reputation and career chock full of accomplishments worthy of a retirement he was contemplating, his old Korean War buddy Colonel William Brodbeck called on Gordon to serve as his executive officer (XO) of the 3rd Brigade, 1st Infantry Division (known as Big Red One) in 1965. On its way to South Vietnam, Big Red One would become one of the first US combat divisions in-country.

So, at the grand old age of forty-one, Gordon stepped up once again to accept the call of his nation and go fight evil forces that would threaten freedom.

Indeed, where does America get such gallant men?

CHAPTER 10

THE AGONY OF VIETNAM

NAM VIET

"The War in Vietnam was a strange war to fight, a stranger war to cover," wrote Hugh Mulligan in his book, *No Place To Die*, published in 1967. Mulligan was an Associated Press writer known by other battle correspondents as the *Ernie Pyle of Vietnam*.

He went on to write;

> Who can remember that it began for America back in President Truman's administration, two years before Dien Bien Phu? Who can remember when it was only an advisory effort, when the American soldiers wore no uniforms, except when they came bouncing out of the old colonial hotels in knapsacks and fatigues to go off to war?
>
> So long ago. And yet, before the decade was out, the cathedral square would be named for a slain American President and the American troop commitment would grow from 350 non-uniformed advisors to about 400,000 men at arms.

Vietnam is a strange land, a bizarre land. The East at its most inscrutable. Also, at its most charming and exciting. Vietnam means "land to the south." Maybe a humorist or a psychologist could make something of the fact that long ago it was called Nam Viet. The past keeps crowding in on Vietnam, a modern country by Asian standards, and keeps turning things around: a water buffalo charges a taxi and knocks it over, and women in coolie hats sit cross-legged by the roadside selling boa constrictors at eight piasters a foot, for eating, while a nearby transistor radio blares the closing New York Stock Exchange prices over AFRS, Armed Forces Radio Service.

The Vietnam War, also known as the Second Indochina War, and to the Vietnamese as the *Resistance War Against America* or simply the *American War*, was a conflict that spread out from Vietnam to Laos and Cambodia from November 1, 1955 through to the fall of Saigon on April 30, 1975. It was officially fought between North Vietnam (proxy of the Soviet Union) and South Vietnam (proxy of the United States of America).

North Vietnam was supported by the Soviet Union and other Communist allies such as China. South Vietnam was supported by the United States, South Korea, the Philippines, Australia, Thailand, Turkey, and other anti-Communist allies.

The war, considered a Cold War-era proxy war by some, lasted nineteen and a half years, with direct US involvement ending in 1973. It included the Laotian Civil War and Cambodian Civil War, which ended with all three countries becoming Communist in 1975.

The conflict emerged from the First Indochina War, pitting the colonial French government against the communist-led Viet Minh. Most of the funding for the French war effort was provided by the United States.

After the French quit Indochina in 1954, the US assumed financial and military support for the South Vietnamese state. The Viet Cong, also known as *Front national de libération du Sud-Viêt Nam* or NLF (the National Liberation Front), a South Vietnamese common front under the direction of North Vietnam, initiated a guerrilla war in the south. North Vietnam also had invaded Laos in the mid-1950s to support insurgents and established the Ho Chi Minh Trail, which was used to supply and reinforce the Viet Cong in South Vietnam.

RAISING THE STAKES

US involvement escalated under Presidents Dwight D. Eisenhower and John F. Kennedy through the Military Assistance Advisory Group (MAAG) program from just under a thousand military advisors in 1959 to sixteen thousand in 1963.

By 1963, the North Vietnamese had sent forty thousand soldiers to fight in South Vietnam. North Vietnam was heavily backed by the USSR and the People's Republic of China. China also sent hundreds of People's Liberation Army (PLA) servicemen to North Vietnam to serve in air defense and support roles.

By the end of 1964, President Lyndon B. Johnson increased the number of US advisors by nearly 50 percent to twenty-three thousand and stationed them throughout South Vietnam.

"A man can fight if he can see daylight down the road somewhere," he told a senator in March 1965. "But there ain't no daylight in Vietnam; there's not a bit." Yet even as he said that, he was committing the first US ground combat units and initiating a massive bombing campaign.

On March 8, 1965, the United States Marine Corps landed 3,500 Marines near Da Nang, South Vietnam. This marked the beginning of the American ground war. I remember one of my Marine Corps Drill Instructors telling us in 1970 that he landed on a beach in Vietnam in 1965, and walked ashore with no weapons. That's how sublime it was in some places at that time.

ESCALATING STRATEGIES

During the controversial Gulf of Tonkin incident in August of that same year, the American patrol boat USS Maddox clashed with Soviet-built North Vietnamese fast attack torpedo boats. In response, the US Congress passed the Gulf of Tonkin Resolution and gave President Johnson broad authority to increase American military presence in Vietnam.

Privately, Johnson himself expressed doubts about the Gulf of Tonkin incident, reportedly confiding in a State Department official that "those dumb, stupid sailors were just shooting at flying fish!" He also questioned the idea of being in Vietnam at all.

Johnson ordered the deployment of combat units for the first time and increased troop levels to 184,000. Past this point, the North Vietnamese Army, or NVA, which had previously embraced guerrilla warfare, stepped up their game and engaged in more conventional warfare with US and South Vietnamese forces.

Despite little progress, the United States continued a significant build-up of forces. US Secretary of Defense Robert McNamara, one of the principal architects of the war, began expressing doubts of victory by the end of 1966 but there was no public retraction of the war effort and it would rage on for another nine years.

Civilian control of the military does have its consequences.

US and South Vietnamese forces relied on air superiority and overwhelming firepower to conduct *search and destroy* operations involving ground forces, artillery, and airstrikes. The US also conducted a large-scale strategic bombing campaign against North Vietnam and Laos.

US public opinion overwhelmingly supported the initial deployments. The marines' assignment was to defend Da Nang Air Base. The first deployment of 3,500 in March 1965 was expanded to include soldiers, sailors, airmen, and more marines to nearly 200,000 by December.

The US military had long been schooled in offensive warfare and was very good at it. Regardless of political policies, US commanders were institutionally and psychologically unsuited to a defensive mission, which is what was called for in Vietnam by successive Presidential administrations of Eisenhower, Kennedy, and Johnson.

AGGRESSIVE DEPARTURE

General William Westmoreland informed Admiral U. S. Grant Sharp Jr., commander of US Pacific forces, that the situation in 1965 was critical. He said, "I am convinced that US troops, with their energy, mobility, and firepower, can successfully take the fight to the National Liberation Front (NLF)." The NLF is an overtly communist party that was established in 1962, but both the military arm—the Viet Cong—and the political organization of the NLF included many non-communists. The NLF was represented by its own diplomatic staffs in all communist countries and in several neutral countries.

With this recommendation, Westmoreland advocated an aggressive departure from America's defensive posture and sidelining of the South Vietnamese Army. By ignoring the Army of the Republic of Vietnam (ARVN) units, the US commitment became open-ended. Westmoreland outlined a three-point plan to win the war:

> Phase 1. Commitment of US (and other free world) forces necessary to halt the losing trend by the end of 1965.

> Phase 2. US and allied forces mount major offensive actions and seize the initiative to destroy guerrilla and organized enemy forces. This phase would end when the enemy had been worn down, thrown on the defensive, and driven back from major populated areas.

Phase 3. If the enemy persisted, a period of twelve to eighteen months following Phase 2 would be required for the final destruction of enemy forces remaining in remote base areas.

The plan was approved by President Johnson and marked a profound departure from the insistence of previous administrations that the government of South Vietnam was responsible for defeating the guerrillas. Westmoreland predicted victory by the end of 1967.

Be careful what you wish for, you just might get it. Hand-in-glove with that warning is to be cautious of predicting an outcome against an unpredictable enemy.

JOHNSON'S DECEPTION

Johnson did not, however, communicate this change in strategy to the media. Instead, he emphasized continuity. The change in US policy depended on matching the North Vietnamese and the VC in a contest of attrition and morale. The US and her opponents were thus locked in a cycle of escalation. The idea that the government of South Vietnam could manage its own affairs was summarily shelved. Westmoreland and McNamara furthermore touted the body count system for gauging victory, a metric that would later prove to be flawed.

The American buildup transformed the South Vietnamese economy and had a profound effect on society. South Vietnam was inundated with manufactured goods. Stanley Karnow noted that "the main PX [Post Exchange], located in the Saigon suburb of Cholon, was only slightly smaller than the New York Bloomingdale's."

A huge surge in corruption was also witnessed. Meanwhile, the one-year American soldier tour of duty deprived front-line units of experienced leadership. As one observer noted, "We were not in Vietnam for ten years, but for one year ten times." As a result, training programs were shortened. In-country experience was limited. Some lessons learned from WWII and Korea were seemingly not heeded.

Meanwhile, the political situation in South Vietnam began to stabilize with the new prime minister Air Marshal Nguyen Cao Ky and figurehead chief of state, General Nguyen Van Thieu. During mid-1965, the military junta propelling them to power seemed to end a series of coups that had occurred previously more than once a year. Although they were nominally a civilian government, Ky was supposed to maintain real power through a behind-the-scenes military body.

However, Thieu outmaneuvered and sidelined Ky by filling the ranks with generals from his faction. Thieu was also accused of murdering Ky loyalists through contrived military accidents.

The Johnson administration had employed a policy of *minimum candor* in its dealings with the media. Military information officers sought to manage media coverage by emphasizing stories that portrayed progress in the war. Over time, this policy damaged the public trust in official pronouncements. As the media's coverage of the war and that of the Pentagon diverged, a credibility gap emerged and public support for the war in Vietnam waned. But in 1965, none of this information was readily available to the general public, so the war was on and the public was in support.

Despite Johnson and Westmoreland publicly proclaiming victory, with Westmoreland stating that the "end is coming into view," internal reports in the Pentagon Papers indicated that VC forces retained strategic initiative and controlled their losses. VC attacks against static US positions accounted for 30 percent of all engagements, with ambushes and encirclements for 23 percent, American ambushes against VC forces for 9 percent, and American forces attacking VC emplacements for only 5 percent of all engagements.

3RD BRIGADE, 1ST INFANTRY DIVISION ARRIVES

Into this caldron of contention, the US Army sent Big Red One to The Republic of Vietnam, where it began five long years of action against this invading army from the communist north. Big Red

One, the 1st Infantry Division with a storied history dating back to WWI, would ultimately earn thirteen battle streamers and citations for its meritorious actions in Vietnam. Into the deep marched Gordon Lippman and the other soldiers of Big Red One, oblivious to President Johnson's deception. Dutifully following their orders to aid and assist the people of South Vietnam, they did their best and some gave their all.

When the first troops arrived, General Westmoreland, Major General Seaman, and Deputy Commanding General Norton were at Vung Tau to greet them.

Echoing the unit's motto, *No Mission Too Difficult, No Sacrifice Too Great—Duty First*, Seaman pledged that "whether this fight will be long or short, we of the *Fighting First* will carry out every mission to a successful completion, whatever the cost or sacrifice."

Code-named *Operation Big Red* after the unit's nickname, the Big Red One began the process of unloading troopships of the division's multitudes of men, equipment, and supplies, bringing them from the docks to the field on October 5, 1965. This complex logistical project lasted until November 2. Coordinated and supervised by the US Army in Vietnam, the operation involved the 1st Logistical Command, the 2nd Signal Group, the 12th Aviation Group, the 716th Military Police Battalion, and the 173rd Airborne Brigade.

Troops were moved to the Vung Tau airfield and then flew on C-130s to Bien Hoa, from where they went by truck to a staging area about halfway between Saigon and Bien Hoa near Saigon University and finally to their base camps.

In the meantime, the small amount of cargo that had accompanied the troopships was loaded onto an LST (landing ship, tank) for transshipment to Saigon. From there, the cargo moved by truck to the staging area. The equipment on the cargo ships followed much the same route.

At the direction of US Military Assistance Command, Vietnam (MACV), the 173rd Airborne Brigade, already in-country for several months, assumed security responsibility for the 1st Division so that it could concentrate on the move and on the establishment of its base camps.

The 173rd already had conducted a two-week operation in the vicinity of Lai Khe (soon to be the new home of the 3rd Brigade) to thwart any disruptions insurgent forces might have planned for that area.

Next, with the assistance of the 2nd Brigade, 1st Infantry Division, which had already been in country for nearly three months, it secured the divisional staging area and began sweeping the division's various base camp locations and the routes to them.

By the end of October, the 173rd had seen the 3rd Brigade, 1st Infantry Division safely to its base area near Lai Khe, and the 2nd Brigade had escorted its sister unit, the 1st Brigade, 1st Infantry Division safely to a site near Phuoc Vinh.

A few days later, the 173rd secured an area near Di An, which would become the base camp for the division's headquarters and support elements.

Toward the end of the month, the 2nd Brigade guarded the movement of division artillery and aviation elements to a base near Phu Loi. These base camps were positioned no more than forty-five kilometers from one another.

The 1st Infantry Division was assigned the duty to both guard the approaches to Saigon from the northwest, north, and northeast, and, from Lai Khe and Phuoc Vinh, and to block enemy movement between War Zones C and D.

In all, Operation Big Red had succeeded in moving over 9,600 troops and their equipment and supplies to their destinations in the III Corps Sector without loss of life or serious injury to anyone.

Upon completion of the operation, the 2nd Brigade returned to the command of its parent unit, and Seaman's 1st Infantry Division was in place, ready to go!

Lai Khe Base Camp was located around sixty kilometers north of Saigon along Route 13 (commonly known as Highway 13). It was a major base and its strategic location meant it played a significant role in III Corps Sector fighting.

Highway 13, also known as Thunder Road, ran through a string of bases that included Lai Khe, north from Saigon.

Lai Khe served as base camp for the 1st Infantry Division, 3rd Brigade Headquarters from 1965-1972, along with several other American units over different periods of time. The Division headquarters were not far away in Di An. Lt. Col. Lippman operated out of Base Camp Lai Khe, which was later renamed in honor of him. The other brigades were stationed at Quan Loi, Phuoc Vinh, and Dau Tieng.

CHAPTER 11

COMBAT OPERATIONS

WITHIN TWO WEEKS OF ARRIVING in Vietnam during July 1965, the 1st Infantry Division began combat operations in the Iron Triangle, which was a long-held VC stronghold. With the VC eager to fight the Americans, these early battles proved noteworthy as lessons learned were useful in preparing the 1st Infantry Division to engage with the North Vietnamese enemy and overcome any obstacles encountered.

Historical reporting tells us just how pervasive the enemy headlock on the area was, as reported in *NAM the Vietnam Experience 65-75*, by Time Page and John Pimlott:

> A dagger pointing directly at Saigon, which was thirty-five miles to the southeast, the Iron Triangle earned its name and reputation long before US forces arrived in Vietnam.
>
> An area of 60 square miles, it was defined by the Saigon River to the southwest, the Thi Tinh River to the east and the Than Dien forestry reserve to the

north to the Bau Long Pond, a distance of about thirteen kilometers. The objective of the operation was to ensure safe passage of the South Vietnamese 5th Division, 7th Regiment over a dangerous stretch of the road on the first leg of its move to the Michelin Rubber Plantation where the Allied unit would conduct a series of search and destroy operations, looking for VC insurgents.

Keeping in accord with the US Army mission in Vietnam at the time, 3rd Brigade had initially provided defense in support of South Vietnamese offensive operations. But as the overall in-country mission began to change to an offensive role, these aggressive battle operations quickly became the norm for US forces.

Seaman handed the assigned mission to the 3rd Brigade commander, Colonel William D. Brodbeck, who in turn assigned the job to Lt. Col. George M. Shuffer's 2nd Battalion, 2nd Infantry Regiment.

Lt. Col. Gordon Lippman, the brigade executive officer (XO), was in charge of coordinating logistics in support of Lt. Col. Shuffer's mission. This included lining up transportation to and from the field, planning for medevac air support, and coordination with artillery and close air support units that would eventually come to Lt. Col. Shuffer's aid. Lieutenant Colonel Lippman and Lieutenant Colonel Shuffer served together as Platoon Leaders and Company Commanders of the 24th Infantry Regiment during the Korean War. Both received Silver Stars and Distinguished Service Crosses for their Korean War service. Both served in combat through WWII, Korea and Vietnam. Lieutenant Colonel Shuffer would go on to become a Brigadier General after his service in Vietnam. A civic affairs team operated during combat operations to provide information management and humanitarian assistance. Some core tasks included identifying non-governmental organizations operating in the battlespace, handling refugee needs, comforting civilians on the battlefield, and identifying protected targets such as schools, churches, temples, and hospitals.

As the 3rd Brigade XO, Gordon's role consisted primarily of watching his commanding officer's (Colonel Brodbeck) back, carrying out his orders, especially in support of combat operations, and ensuring that the brigade companies worked well together and troopers were adequately trained, equipped, and supplied as those needs arose.

His team handled logistics, training, medical aid, personnel, security, and battle group coordination. He also took care of public relations to safeguard the villagers living in areas nearby the base, made sure that they were respected and cared for, and had care packages delivered when available. War correspondents were a constant presence, posing frequent questions and requests for access, which he also fielded and coordinated.

What follows is a description of battle group engagements during the first three significant combat operations for the 3rd Brigade on or near Highway 13, just north of camp. Lt. Col. Lippman provided logistical management and coordination behind the scenes before, during, and after each battle.

Shuffer's men were operating deep into the Iron Triangle, farther north along Highway 13 than any Americans had previously. Unlike the men of the 173rd Airborne Brigade, they had yet to convert to the M16 rifle and were still armed with the slower firing, heavier, but still highly effective, M14.

Lt. Col. Shuffer constructed the task force out of his own unit in addition to Troop A, 1st Squadron, 4th Cavalry, and Battery C, 2nd Battalion, 33rd Artillery. Under his plan the thirteen-kilometer stretch of road was divided into three sectors, with one company-sized unit per sector.

The command group, the battalion's reconnaissance platoon, the 105-mm towed artillery battery, the cavalry troop and Company A went into the middle sector. The other two sectors, one to the north, the other to the south, went to the remaining two companies. Shuffer planned for each unit to sweep its sector during the day. Toward nightfall the three forces would pull into defensive perimeters located at intervals along the highway.

The Americans followed this procedure for two days, November 10 and 11, but other than the uneventful passage of the South Vietnamese 7th Regiment traveling through on their mission, little occurred. The most notable events of the two days were visits by the battalion's civil affairs teams to the hamlets of Ben Dong So and Bau Bang to hand out rice, beans, dry milk, candy, bundles of used clothing, and CARE packages, while gathering useful intelligence on the village.

Following passage of the South Vietnamese regiment, Lt. Col. Shuffer ordered his middle units to establish night defensive positions north and south of Bau Bang.

Having learned on November 10 of the arrival of Shuffer's unit, the VC 9th Division commander, Senior Colonel Hoang Cam, seized the chance to fight Americans, and honed in on Shuffer's command post as his target objective.

During that night Shuffer's middle force received two mortar rounds from the VC, and an ambush that left two VC dead, but most of the time passed in sluggish quiet.

Backed by division mortars and augmented by battalions from the North Vietnamese 271st and 273rd Regiments, the 272nd Regiment led the attack. The 273rd's 9th Battalion would block any attempt by the Americans south of Bau Bang to interfere and its 7th Battalion would stand in reserve.

Colonel Cam's forces prepared for the assault throughout the night. While signalmen laid wire for field telephones around the Americans, other troops slipped into Bau Bang. They positioned mortars within the hamlet itself and dug machine gun and recoilless rifle emplacements into a berm located just to its south, near the new American perimeter.

On the afternoon of November 11, Colonel Cam's forces began to gather for the attack, some of them having marched for up to seven hours to reach Bau Bang.

At 2200, Colonel Cam learned that Shuffer had pulled his task force north of the hamlet, located only 200 meters from the perimeter of the second element in the American middle.

Assuming the risk, the VC Colonel decided to expand his plan and stage an assault that would destroy both American troop concentrations.

To the west and south of the target, hidden by chest-high grass that extended out for about 600 meters or approximately 656 yards, the VC crouched among rubber trees awaiting the order to attack.

To the southeast of the target, more of them assembled near the edge of Highway 13, which ran less than 100 meters to the east of the American perimeter along a level grassy field.

The next morning, on November 12, Shuffer's men were unaware of the approaching enemy force and began preparations to move out on the road, slating their departure for just after 0600.

Colonel Cam pre-emptively launched his attack five minutes after 0600. Although his troops had laid telephone wire, his communications were still so primitive that he had direct contact with only one of his battalions. Cam hoped that when he signaled that battalion to attack, the others would coordinate their actions with the sound of its guns.

For all its flaws, the strategy worked. Over the first ten minutes of the assault, Cam's troops fired approximately fifty mortar rounds into their American targets and then added automatic weapons and small-arms fire.

Meanwhile, the soldiers who had been hiding among the rubber trees made their way through the tall grass to within forty meters of the American perimeter and charged.

Up and alert due to early morning preparations to move out, Shuffer's men responded with deadly effect, quickly boarding armored personnel carriers that roared out to meet the enemy. Mounted with a .50-caliber machine gun and two M60 machine guns, the armored personnel carriers blazed away. The troops onboard fired from open cargo hatches. The American response broke Cam's assault.

The VC had little success in the two attacks that immediately followed.

A fourth attack came at 0700 when the VC, in what probably represented Colonel Cam's main effort, poured south across the berm at Bau Bang and out of a wooded area near the hamlet.

Backed by mortar, recoilless rifle, and automatic weapons fire, they caused some problematic moments for the Americans as a VC suicide squad penetrated their perimeter and threw a grenade into a howitzer position, killing two crewmen and wounding four. In the end, however, these attackers were no more successful than their predecessors.

Reaching the wire, they fell back under the combined weight of the American defenders' artillery, machine guns, and rifles. Especially effective were .55-caliber artillery rounds, howitzers using two-second time fuses, which were fired level to the ground at point-blank range.

American close air support and artillery played a critical role in the outcome of this battle.

Just prior to the 0700 attack, a flight of Air Force A-1H Skyraiders, optimized for ground-attack missions, hit the wooded area to the northwest.

Initially reluctant to fire into Bau Bang itself for fear of killing civilians, Lt. Col. Shuffer's men changed their minds when they realized that the enemy had placed mortars in the hamlet and recoilless rifles on the berm. Soon Shuffer's howitzers were dropping high explosives right on target.

A flight of Navy carrier-based A-4 Skyhawks and another of Skyraiders also arrived, delivering iron bombs, napalm, and cluster bombs that spewed high-velocity pellets upon detonation.

For a while the hamlet was quiet.

Three hours later, at 0900, the surviving VC launched their fifth and final attack.

Once again, American artillery responded, as did a flight of F-100s. As high explosives pounded enemy emplacements and Shuffer's other two companies arrived, the VC withdrew. By 1330, all American positions were secure and the enemy had retreated.

The men of the 2nd Battalion, 2nd Infantry had performed well in their first enemy battle.

TRUNG LOI—BUSHMASTER I

The American 1st Division had a second encounter with a unit from the North Vietnamese 9th Division a little over a week later during *Operation Bushmaster I*. Operating on information that VC had been seen in the Michelin Plantation, South Vietnamese and American commanders ordered a search of the area.

Under Seaman's plan, heavy air strikes would take place south of the plantation on November 14. A short time later the 2nd of the 28th Infantry and the 2nd of the 33rd Artillery moved by convoy from Lai Khe on Highway 13 north to Chon Thanh and turned west toward the plantation on Route 239. Meanwhile, the 1st of the 16th Infantry and the 1st of the 28th Infantry would mount an air-assault southeast of the plantation.

Initially, these two battalions would search east to west from phase line to phase line, while the 2nd of the 28th would function as a blocking force. On the third day, all three infantry battalions maneuvered to the northwest toward a final phase line near the airfield at Dau Tieng.

By November 20, they were done and plans were afoot to return them to base camp at Lai Khe. The 1st of the 16th Infantry moved to Lai Khe by air, but other units including the 2nd of the 28th Infantry, commanded by Lt. Col. George S. Eyster, traveled by motor convoy.

Almost three kilometers in length, the convoy approached the hamlet of Trung Loi, at 1820, which was about eight kilometers short of Highway 13. They came under attack by the VC troops, which were concealed on both sides of the road. With machine gun and small-arms fire raking the road from both sides and with grenades going off, the combat team was pinned down.

As the Americans ran out of ammunition, the VC continued showering them with mortar rounds and grenades.

At that point, Huey gunships were called in and made firing passes from west to east on the southeast side of the road where most of the enemy seemed to be. Next, the gunships made a series of sweeps to drive the ambushers out of their positions onto the roadway where small-arms fire from the convoy killed some of them.

The helicopters departed after ten minutes, but Air Force fighter-bombers were now on the scene, dropping napalm along the southeast side of the road. American and South Vietnamese artillery also zeroed in, bringing the opposite side of the roadway under fire.

By 1900, the robustness of the American response had broken the ambush and within three hours, the battalions started moving again. At 2315 they passed out of the ambush site, arriving at Chon Thanh.

From one standpoint, as General Seaman observed years later, except for the ambush at Trung Loi, the results of Bushmaster I didn't amount to a hill of beans.

From another, however, a valuable operational idea had emerged from the action. According to Seaman, the employment of simultaneous artillery, gunships, and air strikes in support of ground combat had always been a source of trouble.

Following procedures developed in Vietnam between 1962 and 1965, ground-control radar guided strike aircraft to the vicinity of a target. When they would arrive, Air Force officers at the scene took over.

A forward air controller flying a Cessna Bird Dog over the battlefield would describe the target, issue an attack heading, and provide whatever facts he had on artillery fire in the area. With that information, a second controller stationed with the unit on the ground would mark friendly positions by popping smoke grenades.

With the allies identified, the air controller would tag the enemy's positions with smoke rockets and instruct the fighters to begin the attack.

Unless everything was well aligned, the bombing runs could easily intersect the paths of helicopters—medevac, transport, or gunships—supporting the operation. Premature bomb releases by startled pilots might then occur, endangering the lives of friendly troops and civilians.

This same procedure "worked like a charm," according to Seaman as he described the finely tuned Bushmaster I Operation.

NHA MAT—BUSHMASTER II

American operations along Highway 13 and west to the Michelin Plantation continued into December, at which time the month's most notable fight in all of III Corps occurred. The battle at Nha Mat originated during American support of another South Vietnamese operation.

In the early hours of November 27, the 271st and 273rd North Vietnamese Regiments attacked elements of the South Vietnamese 5th Division's 7th Regiment near the plantation.

VC ambush, according to General Seaman, "practically wiped the 7th Regiment out." In response, Seaman ordered Colonel Brodbeck's 3rd Brigade, along with two battalions and artillery, to move in and protect the regiment as it regrouped. On the third day of the operation, Seaman changed Brodbeck's mission. Intelligence indicated that elements of the attacking VC regiments and the Phu Lo Loc Force Battalion might be found southeast of the plantation.

Additionally, late word had arrived that the enemy 9th Division's 272nd Regiment might also be in the area. American units were to move aggressively on offense to exploit this intelligence.

To increase the odds, Seaman assigned a third battalion to Brodbeck's task force to provide security for the brigade command group, while releasing the other two battalions for the chase.

On December 1, *Operation Bushmaster II* began. Two infantry battalions moved to landing zone *Dallas*, inside the Michelin Plantation. The site would function as a staging base for the two battalions and as a command post for the brigade command group.

north. Its corners were anchored on the villages of Ben Cat, Phu Hoa Dong, and Ben Suc. Most of the 6,000 inhabitants lived in Ben Suc. They were later identified by US forces as VC sympathizers and resettled. It was (later) estimated that Ben Suc provided the VC with four rear-service transport companies of soldiers.

Although generally elevated by about forty meters above water level, the Iron Triangle was cut by marshes, swamps, and open rice paddies. There was also densely packed secondary forest, barely penetrated by a few ox-cart roads and foot trails.

Ever since WWII, it had been a refuge for anti-government forces, and by 1965 the area was the HQ of the VC Military Region IV, a staging post for assaults on Saigon.

The Iron Triangle was literally a human anthill, riddled with tunnel and bunker complexes, concealed storage rooms, mined and booby-trapped trails. Two years later, during Operation Cedar Falls, over 1,100 bunkers and 525 tunnels were located and destroyed while the supplies captured included 3,700 tons of rice, 800,000 phials of penicillin, 7500 uniforms, 60,000 rounds of ammunition and hundreds of military documents.

The US Army unwittingly housed 3rd Brigade, 1st Infantry Division right on top of a large portion of this anthill.

BAU BANG

At Bau Bang, the enemy chose the battleground on which to fight.

During November 4, 1965, Major General Pham Quoc Thuan, the South Vietnamese 5th Division Commander, requested that General Seaman's 1st Division secure Highway 13 from Lai Khe

Between December 2 and 5, Brodbeck's task force searched to the southeast of LZ Dallas in a rectangle of jungle and heavy undergrowth that extended about eight kilometers west to east and twenty kilometers north to south. The search area was within the Long Nguyen Secret Zone, which intelligence suggested was being used by the VC as a safe haven.

Following Brodbeck's plan, the two infantry battalions maneuvered methodically over several days from phase line to phase line but failed to find the VC.

Near midday on December 5, Shuffer's 2nd Battalion finally made contact. Just north of the hamlet of Nha Mat and about nine kilometers west of Bau Bang, Shuffer's lead companies came under small-arms, mortar, machine gun, and recoilless rifle fire from bunkers with small-arms fire coming from high up in the surrounding trees.

The encounter soon escalated into a major firefight. Lt. Col. Shuffer sent Company A around the enemy's left flank because it seemed to be the weaker flank, but the VC unit stopped the Americans cold.

Meanwhile, its largest contingent attempted to outflank and attack the Americans on the east side of the road, forcing Company B across the road to the west.

In response, Shuffer deployed his command group along the northern boundary of the emerging US position, establishing what he considered to be the best perimeter defense under the circumstances.

Although pinned down and surrounded by dense jungle, Shuffer had the advantage of firepower. Responding to his requests for support, Col. Brodbeck directed Lt. Col. Lippman to give Lt. Col. Shuffer priority on all available air and artillery support as well as alerting an infantry company to reinforce.

In short order, a battery each from the 1st Division's 8th Battalion, 6th Artillery, and the 23rd Artillery Group's 2nd Battalion, 2nd Artillery, mounting 175mm self-propelled guns, began to lay down heavy fires.

Shuffer also had three helicopter gun teams—made up of two Huey gunships each—at his disposal. In fact, he was so rich in firepower that it posed an organizational challenge. Although believing that the simultaneous employment of his resources would produce the best results, Shuffer had to do it in a way that avoided casualties among his own men. Recalling Trung Loi, he solved the problem by assigning each category of fire support to a clearly designated area.

The sector east of the jungle road went to the Air Force, the area south and southwest to the artillery, and the northern flank of his perimeter to the helicopters. The VC tried to force a postponement of additional fires by moving in close to the Americans, but Shuffer's troops maintained a volume of fire that kept the insurgents at a distance.

Air strikes and artillery bursts laid down a curtain of fire for almost four hours. That protection allowed Company B to hold firm against an assault from the east.

Meanwhile, Companies A and C attacked south into the heart of the enemy bunkers, keeping pace with artillery bursts marching just ahead of them. By 1430, the Americans had penetrated so deeply into the position that the defenders began to lose heart. Running to the rear, the VC left behind not only their dead but also their weapons and equipment.

Shuffer decided against a pursuit because it was late in the day, the size of the enemy force was large but unknown in numbers, and the VC knew the terrain better with much more familiarity on its trails and hiding places than the Americans.

The American troops spent the next several days destroying as much of the bunker system as they could and continued looking for the enemy.

When the mop-up search came up empty, Colonel Brodbeck ruled that the damage done had been sufficient and brought the men back home, ending Bushmaster II.

CHAPTER 12

WELCOME TO ROCKET CITY

BY THE END OF 1965, the 1st Infantry Division had participated in three major operations—Hump, Bushmaster I, and Bushmaster II—under the command of Major General Jonathan O. Seaman.

Lai Khe was a well-chosen site as base camp, right on the highway. Its large runway and relative proximity to Saigon enabled supplies to be brought in fairly easily via both road and air. Another seventy kilometers up the road was a special forces camp located in Loc Ninh. So, protection on Highway 13 northwest of Saigon was easily accessible and well-entrenched.

Being located so close to Saigon meant it was an important part of the city's outer defenses as People's Army of Vietnam (PAVN) forces later in the war would push down Highway 13 during its attacks. At one point, it was one of the most active combative areas when it came to PAVN and VC activities. Being so close to the Iron Triangle, it also meant that many operations were launched from the base, even while it was a constant target for enemy attacks.

Except for the PAVN siege on Khe Sanh, Lai Khe was probably the most rocketed base camp in the country. At times, the camp would receive fifty to seventy-five incoming projectiles during each attack, three times per day and twice at night. There was a sign at the main gate that read: *Welcome to Rocket City.*

Gordon told his family about a Thanksgiving party his unit held for the students of a local high school and added, "I'll send you one of the letters. You might like to show it around as an example of the spirit of the kids in this country who have a chance to speak in freedom."

Reported in an article written by the *Rapid City Journal* on July 20, 1970, is one example of a lesson he learned way back during his time in post-war occupation of Germany. Gordon recognized that after the war comes the peace, and he wanted to initiate that thought process during the conflict.

He was impressed by the appreciation of Ben Cat High School students in Bing Duong. He forwarded the letter that his unit received from the students thanking the 3rd Brigade for their efforts against the VC at Bau Bang. The letter, in beautiful penmanship, which was received by Lippman just two weeks before his own death, said in part:

> You have come from many thousands of miles to our country in the sole purpose of helping our people in the struggle against the communists and fighting for the liberty of the whole free world. We take this opportunity to express to you our sincere admiration and thanks. Next, we want to reserve one minute of reverent silence in memory of those among you who gave their lives for our country's freedom in that Bau Bang battle. We also ask you to convey our sympathy and regrets to those heroes' families in the United States.

Under Lt. Col. Lippman's personal supervision, a sound and effective civic action program was developed and carried out. This accomplishment resulted in the establishment of a close cooperative working relationship with the local Vietnamese communities both in and surrounding the areas from the Brigade base camp.

However, even in this comparatively administrative role, combat sometimes comes too close. The following Associated Press story from November 18, 1965, tells the tale of a curious forty-two-year-old warrior wanting to investigate a surprising set of conditions in an area where just days before (as described in the previous chapter about Bushmaster II), his troops engaged the enemy in heavy fighting.

COPTER KILLS RED TAX COLLECTOR

Lai Khe (Vietnam) (AP)—Death caught up with Viet Cong tax collectors last night on bloody Highway 13. The First Infantry Division was sweeping toward the huge Michelin rubber plantation, 50 miles northwest of Saigon.

Major Roblie Davis, the 3rd Brigade's Air Officer, was climbing into his helicopter for an observation flight when an old Vietnamese man in a coolie hat struggled into camp.

The wispy-bearded peasant had walked for more than two hours to report that a team of Viet Cong tax collectors was stopping all trucks and buses along Highway 13, near Bau Bang, where 146 Communists were killed in severe fighting last Friday.

He told intelligence officers the collectors were demanding 1,000 piasters (about $140) to allow vehicles through.

Dusk was just settling over the endless rows of rubber trees around Brigade headquarters, when Davis took off in his bubble-topped helicopter to have a look. Riding along with him was the Brigade's Executive Officer, Gordon Lippman. Davis' chopper is one of the few bubble-model H13's in Vietnam armed with machine guns.

No one over here thought these choppers could lift those heavy guns until the boys got to experimenting," said Davis explaining his raid on the tax point. He flew in low over the trees and found the three local Communist Commissars sitting at a table near the roadside between a pair of machine guns.

They had quite a business-like operation going on there," said Davis, "sitting right out there in daylight in uniform with web belts on and everything, and traffic backed up for one-quarter of a mile. We swooped down on them and Colonel Lippman let loose with those guns before their machine gunners knew what happened.

We came in so low over the trees, they never saw us coming. On the way out we drew some small arms fire from deep among the trees and a carbine shot the bubble out of my chopper.

Neither Davis nor Lippman were injured when the bubble burst. The maintenance crews had no trouble believing how low they had flown over the trees because they spent an hour picking leaves out of the gun mounts on Davis' ship before getting around to stitching up the plastic bubble."

It looks like Gordon had his hands full, sometimes not getting much sleep for days at a time, plus dealing with an abscessed tooth, so he was probably not in good physical health at the time. A bad tooth can make a person quite ill and irritable. Putting his tooth ache aside, he would often go into battle with his troops, and was not always in the rear with the gear.

In this war zone, it is clear that it can be just as deadly at headquarters as it can in the field. It was discovered much later that brigade headquarters at Lai Khe was positioned right on top of miles of VC tunnels. The VC would crawl out of their tunnels and do a lot of their killing after dark. It's not clear if the brigade ever realized the full extent of the danger in their location. Ben Cat was known for their VC sympathizers. The Iron Triangle was also well known as a major operations area for the VC.

From Gordon's last letter to the family Dec. 6, 1965—just five days before he went home to Glory:

Dearest Family,

Busy, busy, busy. Since we started this operation it's hard to find a minute to breathe. As I mentioned a couple of letters ago—we were committed to go to the Michelin after the 7th ARVN Regiment got chewed up. We didn't get there in time to do them any good— except moral support, but had to stay in the field— close by. After they got their ducks in a row we were ordered to proceed overland in a search and destroy operation back to Lai Khe. This is about the 5th day of that. All resupply, evacuation, command and control must be done by air; hence, coordination required is twice as much and twice as time consuming.

"LTC Shuffer's Battalion (2/2 infantry) ran up on a big enemy force in the middle of a deep jungle yesterday at noon and the fight went to dark. It took the rest of last night and today to get it sorted out, and still have some battlefield to police tomorrow. It cost him about 38 KIAs and 95 WIAs, but he killed 200+ VC and wounded at least that many. It was all bitter and at close range and those are the tough ones—hard to see—hard to move—hard to shoot, etc.

Well, still have a few more days to go on this one so anything can happen (not me, I'm still home, keeping the store).

We got two more infantry battalions and 1 1/2 artillery battalions attached for the operation, so also have our hands full trying to take care of supply and operations for an extra 2,000 people. We look like about 6,000 people. Hard to manage with such a small staff.

Well, I must have gotten 6 or 8 letters and cards from you this past week. About 4 of them were mailed 22 Nov and arrived on 4 December. Other two letters were on Thanksgiving and one today, dated 24 Nov. I feel guilty for not writing more often. Who knows, one day things might slow down so that it will be possible.

Am swamped with the press, trying to get in on last night's battle. This means "stop in the middle of things every hour or so and bring a new group, then try to get them a flight into the battle area and back, etc., etc." They're mostly pretty nice guys so don't mind so much, but it gets on my nerves now and again. Today especially, for I have an abscessed tooth that's bugging me. Haven't really slept except catnap for about 3 nights. Don't have an x-ray machine here so must go to Saigon tomorrow or next day and get it x-rayed. Then can come back here and get it pulled so I don't miss so much work. Once missed, it's murder to catch up.

Have had letters from about everyone in the world. Guess I'll have to give up trying to answer them. Got about a dozen with clippings about that crazy helicopter story. That kind of publicity I really don't need.

Later: Feel better tonight—had a high ball, a good dinner and a shower. Shampooed also, I was tired, hot and filthy dirty—always feel a few years younger when I can get clean again.

Guess this is not really a very good letter. More than

*anything I just wanted you to know I'm still alright—
since I know you will have heard about the last battle.*

*Are you by any chance interested in doing a tour in
Hawaii? Poop sheet out says they will take applications
for duty as PACOM headquarters from people after
tour here is finished. I hear it's awfully hot and humid
most of the time.*

*Our staged Christmas party the other day was
a smashing success. Had 200 kids and all of the
decorations and trimming—including ice cream. You
should see some of this around Christmas in your press.*

*I love you all and miss you more than a whole
bunch. I enjoy your letters—read them all at least twice
and most times more. Sissi certainly wrote a long one
last time. I know you're all busy too, but write when
you can.*

*Love and kisses,
Old Dad*

Captain Jay Franz served with Gordon in Vietnam in the fall
of 1965, and some forty-nine years later he recounted to me what
transpired on that night of December 11, 1965. The incident and the
man left such an indelible impression on the young captain, that he
was able to vividly tell the story of Gordon's last moments on Earth.

Franz is now himself a retired lieutenant colonel, having served
in the Army for twenty-eight years. He had minimal interaction with
Gordon on the troop ship transporting the brigade from the United
States to Vietnam, but more interaction in country once they arrived.

This is his recollection as one of the last soldiers to have spoken
with Gordon before he passed. I think this offers an interesting view
into the man and leader that Gordon was, as well as some of the
intricacies and pleasantries of an Army in the field:

Colonel Lippman was the commander of troops on the troop ship USNS *Daniel Sultan,* on which we shipped over to Vietnam, so I knew of him but had no direct contact on the ship. I was a captain commanding C (Charlie) Company, 1st Engineer Battalion, which would be assigned to support the 3rd Brigade, 1st Infantry Division, in Vietnam. Lt. Col. Lippman was the executive officer (XO) of that brigade.

We were at sea for a few weeks before disembarking and moving to our encampment in Lai Khe during October 1965. This was on an old French rubber plantation. There were a few buildings that had apparently served as offices for the plantation, and a substantial villa which had been the residence of the plantation manager.

The latter became the quarters for the brigade commander and his staff while the headquarters was set up in the former office buildings. My engineers performed construction missions ranging from providing wooden tent floors for all the brigade units to improving a crude landing strip so it could handle USAF C-130s.

As combat engineers, my men were also detailed to accompany infantry units on their operations. These men would normally provide mine detection and clearance but also served as additional infantrymen.

Staff meetings at the brigade level were a daily occurrence. At one of these meetings in early November my XO (a 1st lieutenant) represented me in my absence. After that meeting, he told me that one of the infantry battalion commanders (a lieutenant colonel) had claimed during the meeting that the engineers had gotten lumber with which to construct tent floors but were flooring their own tents before distributing the floors to other units.

Later that day I saw Lt. Col. Lippman driving through my area in his jeep and approached him to find out if I could be of assistance. He said he was just driving through, and asked me if we had flooring in any of our tents. I reported that we did not. He thanked me and drove on.

At the next staff meeting, where my XO again represented me, Lt. Col. Lippman informed the other Lt. Col. that his information was incorrect, that the engineers did not have any flooring in their tents and that he should go make a personal apology to the engineer CO.

That battalion commander, whose name I don't recall, drove over to our area and grudgingly apologized for his incorrect accusation. This meant a great deal to the men in my unit, and showed what kind of man Gordon was.

A few days later, following another staff meeting, Lt. Col. Lippman invited me to have dinner at the brigade commander's quarters that evening. Being naïve, I asked what the appropriate uniform would be. Before leaving Fort Riley we were required to pack a number of items, including our dress blue uniforms, in our duffel bags. Lt. Col. Lippman said the uniform would be dress blues; then, after seeing my reaction, quickly said he was joking and the regular combat uniform was to be worn.

The brigade commander (Colonel Brodbeck), because of his rank and position, was provided an enlisted aide who served as chef, and the dining room had regular silverware and linen tablecloth and napkins. After weeks of very drab rations eaten in drab surroundings, dinner seemed very elegant.

As I recall, there were about eight of us at the dinner table; there was one other guest besides me. The others—brigade staff officers—all lived there in the colonel's quarters. The brigade commander also had a group of military police who served as his bodyguard; this was routine.

During the meal we could hear gunfire on the perimeter. This was an almost daily occurrence, where the VC would fire a few rounds into the brigade area after nightfall just to remind us they were there. On this night, the gunfire lasted longer than usual.

After a while, Gordon announced that he was going to go check on "the boys"—his reference to the MP's guarding the colonel. He put on his web gear and shortly after he left the quarters, we heard someone shout that "the colonel's been hit." We all scrambled to go assist; because my web gear was most accessible, I was the first to leave the building.

As I was leaving, I drew my .45 in anger for the first time since being in-country and began searching for the colonel. It was dark now and when I found him, it was obvious that he was seriously injured and he was in a lot of pain.

On learning that radio communications between the colonel's quarters and headquarters were temporarily out, I ran for my jeep and drove to HQ to notify the medics that Lt. Col. Lippman was wounded. That trip proved unnecessary. The medics had somehow gotten the word and soon they brought Gordon into one of the HQ buildings.

In a rare circumstance, a medevac helicopter was

parked near the brigade HQ. I think darkness had overtaken the pilot and he'd decided to remain at Lai Khe overnight. I and others thought that was a good omen, since it meant Gordon would be at a hospital in much less time than under normal circumstances.

While the medevac helicopter was being readied for takeoff, Gordon said his final farewells to the commander and the rest of us. He was in great pain, but spoke clearly and movingly, saying it had been an honor to serve with us. He also said he knew he would not be back. When he was finally carried out on a litter to the waiting helicopter, we were quite optimistic.

Early the following morning we learned that he had passed away, either during the flight or soon after arriving at the hospital in Saigon. The news was devastating. I didn't know anyone who did not hold him in the highest regard.

Lt. Col. Gordon Joseph Lippman laid in state for twenty-four hours at the Ives Funeral Home in Arlington, Virginia, after arrival by plane from Vietnam. With a military escort, using the same caisson that carried President John F. Kennedy, he was buried with full military honors at Arlington National Cemetery in Washington, DC.

CHAPTER 13

LEGACY

HUMOR

Gordon was very much like his mother. His parents had moved from Lemmon to Hill City, South Dakota, in 1947. She was a dynamo, getting to know everyone in Hill City and they got to know her. Arleen was their biggest champion!

Arleen with Julie

Arleen was always busy with one thing or another, and is one of the local Chamber of Commerce members granted a lifetime membership. She was, at age eighty, a member of the Guinness Book of World Records as a participant in the longest chorus line in the world at that time.

She was involved in crafts, fairs, and parades. This photo shows her enjoying a laugh with her great-granddaughter, Julie Flounders. Arleen is wearing a colonial era uniform that she sewed herself. She wore it while playing fife in the Hill City Fife and Drum Corps.

Gordon found the humor in life but

dismissed folly—a crucial life-lesson learned from his maternal Grandmother Swan. A devoutly religious woman, she taught him to enjoy life. His leadership style showed that it was okay to be witty but not silly; fun but not foolish; good natured but not conceited.

The friendships he established and collaboration with others left a legacy of a firm but fair leader. The friendship he had with Bing Crosby and Bob Hope was just one such example. While serving as the 3rd Brigade XO in Lai Khe, Bing Crosby had asked Gordon to play a prank on his old buddy Bob Hope during an upcoming USO Show.

Among his other official duties, Gordon had been working diligently to coordinate a Bob Hope USO Christmas Show that was scheduled to visit the Lai Khe area during the upcoming holidays. In addition to Gordon's role as master of ceremonies, he was to play the straight man in a Bing Crosby-scripted prank, presenting Hope with the photo and a remark from Crosby. Crosby, who had battled wits with Hope for years, had sent a photograph and letter to Gordon, an old friend, containing cracks at "Ample Robert." In the letter Crosby said he hoped Gordon would have fun when Ample Robert appeared at his billet. Crosby went on to say, "I know he'll be a big hit there—I've been working hard with him, getting him up in his material, and on his delivery, cleaning up his act a bit, and sprucing it up where it needed some lively interpolations." The photograph showed Bing following through a golf stroke. In one corner was the inscription: "Dear Bob, don't you wish you had a finish like this? And a waistline? Love, Bing." He ended the letter saying he had profound admiration for all the men in Vietnam and appreciated the tough conditions under which they served.

Following news of Gordon's untimely death, the USO Show was redirected to another area to entertain the troops, since Lai Khe had become a hotbed of enemy activity. On hearing the sad news about their friend, both Crosby and Hope subsequently wrote personal letters expressing their condolences to the Lippman family.

Leadership, bravery, courage, honor, integrity, loyalty, and duty were evident throughout his career and his life.

As we have seen repeatedly, Gordon's leadership and bravery were constantly on display in one combat situation after another. He showed in France and Belgium, during WWII, that the fundamental lessons taught by his parents and grandparents served him well when life-and-death decisions weighed in the balance of is actions.

Although he never attended West Point, the Army's military academy motto—duty, honor, country—was a precept held firmly by Gordon throughout his career and may have been instilled in him by his old battalion commander twenty-two years earlier.

His troopers didn't just need him to lead them, they *wanted* him to lead them. His peers also recognized and welcomed his leadership. No jealousy, just admiration and respect for the man.

THE ANSWER

As this writer has questioned many times throughout this book, where does America get such gallant men? Gordon proved one more time that his WWII training and experiences stuck with him throughout a distinguished twenty-two-year career.

He never shrank from his responsibilities, and in fact he embraced the concept of *lead, follow, or get out of the way*. As he learned from Lt. Col. "Wild Bill" Boyle at the Soy-Hotton Road engagement and with his display of unselfish courage in the face of North Korean machine gunners, Gordon continually developed and refined his skills through every year of his dedicated service. He led *all the way*—from the front!

His parents and grandparents were from humble beginnings in small town America. He was instilled with honorable character traits and found good mentors to follow along the way. It takes a special human being to remember his roots in the midst of chaos. Gordon showed the way, all the way, from Lemmon, South Dakota!

IN THE COMPANY OF HEROES

According to *South Dakota Magazine*, the state of South Dakota has produced some amazing veterans. Jean Mehegan, founder of

Medary Acres greenhouse in Brookings, survived the Japanese attack on Pearl Harbor. Don Smith of Belle Fourche was a member of Doolittle's Raiders, which launched the first retaliatory attack against Japan following their surprise attack on Pearl Harbor.

Walter Herrig taught in SDSU's Army ROTC program but was first a prisoner of war for much of the WWII conflict. He was captured by the Japanese on the island of Corregidor in 1942. Clarence Wolf Guts was one of the famed Lakota code talkers who suffered unnecessary prejudice as a Native American in a White man's Marine Corps while helping to win the brutal Pacific island-hopping campaign.

Joe Foss was a United States Marine Corps Major and a leading Marine fighter ace in World War II. He received the Medal of Honor in recognition of his role in air-to-air combat during the Guadalcanal Campaign.

In postwar years, he rose to the rank of Air National Guard Brigadier General, served as the twentieth Governor of South Dakota (1955–1959), President of the National Rifle Association (NRA), and was the first commissioner of the American Football League.

Gordon Lippman was one of those South Dakota men. He tasted his first combat action at the age of eighteen in Italy and participated in one of the key parachute jumps of World War II into southern France, leading his men through Belgium and Germany before he had even graduated from high school! He led a segregated Black company through Korea in the freezing rain and mud of the winter at the age of twenty-seven, and at forty-two he led a new generation of warriors into the thick jungles of Vietnam.

Where does America get such gallant men? Why do men like "Wild Bill" Boyle, George Rumsey, Bud Biddle, Willie Robinson, Asia Peterson, Lyle Rishell, Jay Franz, and Gordon Lippman, knowing the horror and fear of what combat is really like, walk back into combat again and again?

To do what is right!

EPILOGUE

IF YOU TAKE AWAY JUST one lesson learned from this story, let it be to do the very best you can at whatever you choose to do with your life, with the gifts God has given to you. Don't complain. Don't shy away from the hard work. In your own way, fight for what is right.

If you're a Christian, then do everything to the best of your ability for the glory of the Lord.

If you work for a corporation, non-profit organization, religious organization, or government agency, give your very best each and every day to the betterment of your organization. If you're a spouse and parent, devote yourself to giving all you have to your family. And if you have children, selflessly do what's right for them! If you're serving in the military, commit yourself to loyalty, respect, safety, well-being, and excellence for your fellow soldier, sailor, marine or airman.

If you drive a truck, become the best, most courteous, on-time driver on your team. If you teach, do it with zeal. If you're a journalist, report your stories truthfully and with integrity, relying solely on the facts not on an opinionated agenda. If you're a first responder, serve your community honorably and respectfully.

Gordon was a man's man, a soldier's soldier—a true patriot in the best sense of the word. Because he inspires me so much and is so much better than me, he is my hero, and has encouraged me to be the best I can be, to do what is right!

MEMORIES FROM THE FAMILY

FROM SON, MARK LIPPMAN:

Dad had incredible patience with us kids, as he and Lucille adopted all three of us. So that says a little about their character. They adopted Lura first. Their original intent was to have a son and daughter.

When they adopted me, I was about three or four. The adoption agency did not tell them I had a brother. When they found out, they took Mike also, to keep us together.

While stationed in Washington DC, we had an awesome house and big yard. Each weekend we would have the neighborhood kids come and play ball. Dad was always there to help all to learn and have fun. After playing ball he would pack all the kids in our old station wagon and drive out for ice cream.

As he was leaving us for Vietnam (I was 10 or 11), I grabbed his pant leg and tried to stop him. He lovingly picked me up and said he had to go to war so I would not have to, when I grew up.

He was a loving and kind father. Never raised a hand on us. That was Mom's job, and oh boy could she wing ding me from time to time. (I deserved and earned each one).

I have tried to emulate his ways in my life with the goal to be half the man he was. Still working on that part.

Everyone respected and loved him.

FROM DAUGHTER, LURA (LIPPMAN) WELLER:

I had a very hard time with his death and was even put back a year in school because of it. I do remember going to my Mom's family farm in Kansas in the summer. We always had a great time at the Twin Lakes my grandparents were caretakers of.

I remember when I had to go to an eye specialist in Winchester, Virginia. He would always let me take my live bunny with me because I wanted it to go along. He loved his family very much. I was always very much a daddy's girl. I have a KIA bracelet that I wear all the time and have had for many years.

FROM SON, MIKE LIPPMAN:

I have many fond memories of Dad, even if we were only together as a whole family for a short time (six years). But it was always quality time. Prior to our move to Fort Riley with the 1st Infantry Division, Dad built a tree house for us in the backyard of our Vienna, Virginia, home, where we spent many hours having dirt clod fights, swinging on a tire below the tree house, and playing war and army.

He commuted to work at the Pentagon from this home. We even had a military regulation tent that he put up. We kids wanted to sleep in it, and tried, but it had the odd military smell which was so strong for our recruit noses that we could not sleep and we ended up back inside the house!

Dad smiled and said it was a new tent that had the military impregnated waterproofing. We played badminton, rode bikes, and picked wild blackberries which always required body tick checks afterwards.

There was a trail that ran along the street in front of our house, hidden from the road by some trees. I remember we would ride down that trail, grabbing hold of a low branch and letting the bike continue on to see how far and where it would go. During my turn, my bike went out into the road. However, I didn't notice the car coming and it was hit and destroyed. Needless to say. My bike-riding was over for the summer. Not sure I would have been able to sit on one for a while anyway!

I remember on occasion I would fall asleep downstairs and Dad would pick me up and carry me up to bed. I could have walked but I really liked being carried, so I faked being asleep.

Also, another bold incident that comes to mind—it's about Dad and how he galvanized our personal bond. Just prior to his departure for Vietnam in the summer of 1965, we had a family picnic at the Council Grove Twin Lakes, where my Grandfather Lee Meier was caretaker. Dad was sitting in the pavilion near the water reading a book and keeping an eye on us kids in the water.

We were floating on blow up rafts just beyond the floating boat dock which would hold about four or five boats. It was a place where much time was spent and many great memories were made, great for fishing and diving, etc. I think everyone knows of a place like this.

I remember I was laying on my raft face up and had dozed off, letting my guard down. All of a sudden, I woke up under water. My brother, the prankster, not realizing I was asleep, had quietly floated over and pulled the raft out from under me.

As I came up gasping for air, getting my bearings, splashing and yelling at Mark, I saw Dad running full sprint down the boat dock, diving into the water, clothes, wallet, watch and all. I remember saying, "I'm okay! I'm okay!" But he still swam like a man on a mission to save me. Needless to say, swimming was over for the day. But I was proud of him, just one of the examples of why he will always be my favorite hero.

Earlier in 1965 I was in the cellar of our Vienna home with Dad while he was packing his foot lockers. I remember saying I did not want him to go to Vietnam because I was worried he would not come back. I think that shocked him a bit. He reassured me all would be okay and that he was going so that someday we would not have to. He sent me away upstairs so he could pack in peace.

I guess I was a bit intuitive as a nine-year-old. When we took him to the airport to go overseas in September, he gave us kids each a dollar to get a soda. When we went back to see him off, he had already boarded. Not sure of the exact moment we kids said goodbye but I'm sure it happened.

I understand he also wanted a private moment to say goodbye to Mom. It was very quiet in the car driving home. In his first letter home he said he had a lump in his throat when the plane took off.

I'm not sure of the exact date in December, but it was in1965 while in Council Grove, during the evening on a Saturday. Mom, Lura, Mark, and I were watching *Gunsmoke*. I was laying on the couch and was distracted by a disturbing premonition that something had happened to Dad. This was very close to the date he was killed in action (Dec. 11, 1965). More intuition perhaps.

It was not long after when a priest came into our bedroom in the middle of the night. He went to the closet, turned the light on, and said "Boys! Get up, you have a crisis on your hands."

It all seemed unreal . . . being awakened into a nightmare. Mom needed us up.

I remember going downstairs and seeing mom in her bedroom, crying tears I will never forget. We kids sat in the living room stunned. It was just all a bad dream. I suppose in a way it still is. But I do know this, I am eternally proud of him!

FROM GORDON'S COUSIN, GAIL WELLS:

I remember in 1948 when Gordon and his wife, Lucille, drove through Valley City on their way to visit his parents in South Dakota. They had stopped to visit mother, who was his aunt. Mom let me go with them and spend a couple of weeks at his parents' home in Hill City. I was about fifteen-years old at the time.

Gordon was very respectful to everyone, including me. He was calm and laid back and definitely stood out as someone special on that old homestead. Newton Fork Ranch at that time consisted of their small home. It had no indoor plumbing, had a hand-pump in the kitchen, and a large rolling field, wild with growth.

Arleen adored Gordon and he would sit for hours on the back porch chatting with his Dad, Harold. Before departing for Valley City, he bought a new wardrobe for Lucille, specifically for this trip to visit family in the Black Hills of South Dakota, and she was thrilled about it!

He took us all to Mount Rushmore one day, and he seemed very dignified for such a young guy. Gordon and Lucille were a good-looking couple. They would have been in their mid-twenties at that time. She was pretty and he was handsome.

When it was time for me to go back home to Valley City, Gordon took me into Hill City and rented a hotel room for me, because the bus didn't leave until early the next day. So, he paid for the room, told me how to block the door so I'd feel safe. He asked the hotel clerk to call me in the morning and told me where to find the bus. Then he and Lucille left on their drive back to Fort Benning, Georgia, as he was due to report for duty. I came away with the impression of him that he quietly engaged people in dialogue, was patient, kind, helpful, instructive.

FROM GORDON'S NIECE, PATRICE (LIPPMAN) SWOFFORD:

Gordon and Lucille insisted that our family come to Kansas and live with them to make a new start after my parents' divorce. Uncle Gordon sent his personal car and driver to pick us up at the airport as we flew in from California.

Through the years my mother and Lucille were in regular contact via phone. My impression of Gordon is that he was an honored military man and an exemplary human being. I am grateful that he thought enough of his brother's family to step in and offer us a home. In any conversations where Gordon's name was mentioned I have never heard anyone utter a negative word about him . . . quite the legacy.

FROM GORDON'S COUSIN, LINDA FLOUNDERS:

He was a saint. He was respected and admired by every family member I knew.

This testimonial about Gordon would not be complete without some insight on his lovely wife, Lucille. Following below are some memories from Mark, Lura Lee, and Mike about their mother.

FROM LURA LEE (LIPPMAN) WELLER:

Lucille strived for perfection and achieved it when entertaining.

FROM MARK LIPPMAN:

Mom was an excellent hostess and entertainer. She loved to cook and have parties. As an officer's wife she took that role very seriously. She would arrange many formal dinners and parties. She also worked part-time in real estate sales.

I believe she really enjoyed these activities. She also strongly encouraged us kids to be a part of these activities. We saw many, many days of polishing silverware and training in good manners. The social part of being an officer's wife was a serious part of her make up.

She also handled all discipline with us children. We can laugh about it now, but you mess up and that wonderful, petite woman would provide a *wing ding* that could make your head ring for hours. Mine were all well deserved.

In those days, long before cell phones, we were taught to answer the telephone very properly: "Hello, this is the residence of Lieutenant Colonel Lippman. Mark Lippman speaking. How may I help you?"

FROM MIKE LIPPMAN:

For entertaining formal social events, Lucille was an excellent hostess but she needed an assistant, to allow her the opportunity to entertain with Gordon as his wife and attend to guests personally while not being confined to the kitchen.

However, Mom would personally replenish the hors d'oeuvre trays, silver plated punch bowl, etc., when necessary. In Vienna, she hired a maid named Caroline, who came occasionally to help with the daily home cleaning tasks; ironing, cooking, etc., and helped in the kitchen for the parties. Lucille personally prepared many of the hors d'oeuvres but some food was catered.

She was an excellent cook and baker. She had many specialties like lasagna, beef stew, and Country Captain. After moving to Carlisle, she continued to entertain military friends she had met at the Carlisle Barracks Officers Club, as well as neighbors and other nonmilitary friends.

She had another maid named Mrs. Minick who assisted in the same manner mentioned earlier. She also hired a bartender who worked at the officers club on post. With the basement finished off, there was a nice bar, and a main gathering and entertainment space.

In Carlisle, we kids made an appearance long enough to meet the guests but did not mingle long with the adults. We did sample the spiked punch when no one was looking!

GORDON'S MEDALS, AWARDS, AND PATCHES

MEDALS AWARDED, IN ORDER OF IMPORTANCE:

- **Army Distinguished Service Cross—** Awarded to Gordon for distinguishing himself by extraordinary heroism in the vicinity of Do Chung, Korea on 11 April 1951. While engaged in an action against an enemy of the United States, he led his company against entrenched enemy machine gunners. This act of heroism was so notable and involved risk of his life that was extraordinary as to set him apart from his comrades.

- **Army Distinguished Service Medal—** Awarded to Gordon while serving with the United States Army, distinguishing himself by exceptionally meritorious service above and beyond normal duty, to the government in a great responsibility. The performance was such as to merit recognition for service that was clearly exceptional. Exceptional performance of normal duty will not alone justify an award of this decoration.

- **Silver Star, with Oak Leaf—**The third-highest personal decoration by the United State Army for valor in combat. The Silver Star Medal was awarded to Gordon for gallantry in action against an enemy of the United States. The second award of the Silver Star Medal is denoted by a bronze oak leaf cluster.

- **Legion of Merit—**Awarded to Gordon for exceptionally meritorious conduct in the performance of outstanding services and achievements in the Republic of Vietnam from 11 Aug 1965 to 11 Dec 1965. The decoration is issued to members of the eight uniformed services of the United States as well as to military and political figures of foreign governments.

- **Bronze Star, with 2 Oak Leaf Clusters—** Awarded to Gordon for heroic service in a combat zone (during WWII's Battle of the Bulge and the second on 29 June 1944 in Germany). The medal is awarded by the Army and Air Force for acts of valor in combat, The medal requires a recommendation by the commander and a citation in orders. For the six Korean War campaigns he was a part of, Gordon was awarded six more Oak Leaf Clusters

- **Purple Heart, with two Oak Leaves—** Awarded to Gordon in the name of the president, for two separate combat wounds received in Korea, and his death in combat while serving in Vietnam. With its forerunner, the Badge of Military Merit, which took the form of a heart made of purple cloth, the Purple Heart is the oldest military award still given to US military members and was initiated by General George Washington.

- **Air Medal (Army/Air Force)—**Awarded to Gordon for his combat jump during Operation Dragoon in Southern France. During World War II, the medal's award criteria varied widely depending on the theater of operations, the aircraft flown, and the missions accomplished. In Europe, the airspace was considered completely controlled by the enemy and heavy air defenses were encountered.

- **Army Commendation Medal, with Oak Leaf**—Awarded to Gordon while distinguishing himself for meritorious service during the period 1 August 1956 to 31 July 1957 while serving as CO Company H, 5th Infantry Regiment, 8th Infantry Division. The Oak Leaf Cluster was awarded for distinguishing himself for meritorious service during the period 1 May 1958 to 31 May 1959 as the assistant to the chief of staff and assistant plans officer (G-3) Headquarters, 8th Infantry Division.

- **Army Good Conduct Medal**—Awarded to Gordon for sustained acts of heroism or meritorious service. Each branch of the United States Armed Forces issues its own version of the Commendation Medal, with a fifth version existing for acts of joint military service performed under the Department of Defense.

- **American Campaign Medal**—Awarded to Gordon for performing military service in the American Theater of Operations during World War II.

- **European/African/Middle Eastern Campaign, with Oak Leaf and Star—** Awarded to Gordon for recognition of his performance of military duties in the European Theater (including North Africa and the Middle East) during the years of the Second World War. Gordon participated in combat campaigns in Italy, France, Belgium, and Germany.

- **World War II Victory Medal—** Awarded to Gordon for participating in the successful war victory over the Axis Powers in World War II.

- **Army of Occupation Medal (Awarded from 1945–1990)—** Awarded to Gordon for his part in performing occupation service in Germany following WWII. His service included deployments immediately after the war concluded and for a time following his Korean War service in the 1950s.

- **National Defense Service Medal (Awarded from 1950–1954)**—Awarded to Gordon for his service during this period. Combat or in theater service is not a requirement for the award.

- **Korea Service Medal, with Oak Leaf and Star**—Awarded to Gordon for his military service in Korea.

He was authorized the following campaign stars to be added to his Korean Service Medal:

UN Defensive June 27—Sept 15 1950
UN Offensive Sept 16—Nov 2 1950
CCF Intervention Nov 3 1950—Jan 24 1951
1st UN Counteroffensive Jan 25—Apr 21 1951
CCF Spring Offensive Apr 22—July 8 1951
UN Summer—Fall Jul 9—Nov 27 1951

- **Vietnam Service Medal, with Star**—were awarded to Gordon to recognize his service during the Vietnam War.

- **French Croix De Guerre WWII—** Awarded to Gordon's unit, the 517th Parachute Regimental Combat Team, for their meritorious service in helping to liberate France from German occupation during Operation Dragoon.

- **Belgium Croix De Guerre WWII—** Awarded to Gordon's unit, the 82nd Airborne Division, for their meritorious service in helping to liberate Belgium during the Battle of the Bulge.

- **Vietnam Gallantry Cross with Palm Individual Citation—**Awarded to Gordon by the former Government of South Vietnam (Republic of Vietnam). The medal is in recognition of his heroic conduct while in combat with the enemy.

- **United Nations Service Medal (Korea)**—Awarded to Gordon by the United Nations. The decoration was the first international award ever created by the United Nations and recognized the multi-national defense forces which participated in the Korean War.

- **Republic of Vietnam Campaign Medal**—Awarded to Gordon for his service in South Vietnam. It was awarded to members of United States, Australian, and New Zealand military forces serving six months or more in support of Republic of Vietnam military operations.

- **Vietnamese Civic Action 1st Class**—Awarded to Gordon by the former South Vietnamese government (1955–75) for his civic action in support of public education for Vietnamese school children near Lai Khe.

- **Republic of Korea War Service Medal**—Awarded to Gordon by South Korea to recognize members of a military who served with South Korea during the Korean War from June 25, 1950–July 27, 1953.

- **Combat Infantry Badge, with 2 Stars**—Awarded to Gordon for a minimum of thirty days in combat during each of the following  qualifying wars. The National Infantry Museum has a memorial to the soldiers who have been awarded three CIBs in the course of their Army careers. There were only 325 recipients at the time of Gordon's third award. Over his twenty-two-year army career, Gordon served for more than a total of 700 days in combat wearing the uniform.

  1. **World War II** (7 December 1941 to 3 September 1945).
  2. **Korean War** (27 June 1950 to 27 July 1953).
  3. **Vietnam War and other operations** (2 March 1961 to 10 March 1995).

- **Master Parachutist**—was awarded to Gordon for his combat jump into Southern France during Operation Dragoon. To be eligible for the Master Parachutist Badge, an individual must

have been rated excellent in character and efficiency and have met the following requirements:

- Participated in a minimum of sixty-five jumps, including twenty-five jumps with combat equipment. Four night-jumps must also be made during the hours of darkness, one as jumpmaster of a stick. Five mass tactical jumps must be made which culminate in an airborne assault problem with a unit equivalent to a battalion or larger.

- Graduated from the Jumpmaster Course of the Airborne Department of the Infantry School or the Jumpmaster School of a separate airborne battalion or larger airborne unit containing organic airborne elements, or served as jumpmaster on one or more combat jumps or as jumpmaster on thirty-three noncombat jumps.

- Have served on jump status with an airborne unit for a total of thirty-six months (may be non-consecutive).

- The twenty-five combat-equipment jumps necessary to qualify for the Master Parachutist Badge must be from a static line.

- **Army Presidential Unit Citation—**
Awarded to the 82nd Airborne Division for extraordinary heroism in actions against Axis Powers (Germany and Italy) during WWII. The unit displayed such gallantry, determination, and *esprit de corps* in accomplishing its mission under extremely difficult and hazardous conditions so as to set it apart from and above other units participating in the same campaign.

♦ **Korean Presidential Unit Citation**—Awarded to the 24th Infantry Regiment by the government of South Korea  for outstanding performance in defense of the Republic of Korea. In recognition of allied military service to South Korea during the Korean War, all United States military departments were authorized the unit award for that period.

UNITS IN WHICH GORDON SERVED:

517th Parachute Infantry Regiment

2nd Battalion, 505th Parachute Infantry Regiment

82nd Airborne Division

505th Airborne Infantry Regiment

504th Airborne Infantry

24th Infantry Regiment

1st Battalion, 34th Infantry Regiment

Infantry Center and School (Staff) Fort Benning, GA

104th Infantry Division (Timber Wolves)

Command and General Staff College (CGSC) Course

8th Infantry Division

61st Infantry Regiment

5th Infantry Division

2nd Airborne Battle Group, 503rd Infantry

Armed Forces Staff College (Staff)

Department of the Army

National War College

3rd Brigade, 1st Infantry Division

OTHER OFFICIAL AWARDS:

Army Staff Identification:

Infantry Shoulder Cord—During the Korean War General "Lightning Joe" Collins, Chief of Staff for the Army, asked a group of advisors what could be done to enhance the morale of the fighting Infantryman. It was decided that they would receive special insignia, so that everyone would know that the soldier was an Infantryman who would be fighting on the front lines. A light-blue cord was created to be worn over the right shoulder of both officers and enlisted men.

Aide-de-Camp Aiguillette—Within the United States Army, *aides-de-camp* are specifically appointed to General-grade officers (NATO Code OF-6 through OF-10). The usual tour of duty for aides is up to two years.

WWII Honorable Service Lapel Button—The Honorable Service Lapel Button, sometimes called the Honorable Service Lapel Pin, was awarded to United States military service members who were discharged under honorable conditions during World War II. The Department of Defense awarded the button between September 1939 and December 1946.

Associations:

Legion of Valor—Gordon was inducted into the Legion. It is a federally chartered corporation created to promote patriotic allegiance to the United States and fidelity to the US Constitution, as well as popular support for civil liberties and the permanence of free institutions. Its membership is open to recipients of the Medal of

Honor, the Distinguished Service Cross, the Navy Cross and the Air Force Cross. More information can be found at www.legionofvalor. com.

Vietnam Veterans Memorial—Honoring the men and women who served in the controversial Vietnam War, the Vietnam Veterans Memorial chronologically lists the names of 58,318 Americans who gave their lives in service to their country. Gordon Joseph Lippman's name is on Panel 04E, Line 012 of the Vietnam Veterans' Memorial Wall in Washington, D.C.

The National Gold Star Family Registry—The National Gold Star Family Registry is a program of Military Families United, a 501c3 Non-Profit organization that does not endorse or promote *any* political candidate for any political office. The use of a name such as *Gold Star Family* is commonly used to describe a family whose immediate family member was killed in action.

Colleges Attended:

University of Maryland University College, University of North Carolina at Chapel Hill, Army Staff College, University of Omaha, Georgetown University, National War College

RESOURCES

1st Infantry Division. https://en.wikipedia.org/wiki/1st_Infantry_
Division_(United_States)#Vietnam

1st Inf Div: Historical *Study on the Deployment of the 1st Infantry
Division to Vietnam*, 67A/5293, RG 319, NARA.

1st Division, p. 55; People's Army of Vietnam, 2(bk. I, ch.3):1;

24th Infantry Regiment. https://www.historynet.com/korean-war-
forgotten-24th-and-34th-infantry-regiments.htm

24th Infantry Regiment. https://www.25thida.org/units/
infantry/24th-infantry-regiment/#Korea

517 Parachute Regimental Combat Team: http://517prct.org/
documents/odyssey/odyssey_history.htm

517th Parachute Regimental Combat Team. https://en.wikipedia.
org/wiki/517th_Parachute_Regimental_Combat_Team

517 PRCT Association: http://517prct.org/association.htm

AAR, Operation HUMP, 173d Abn Bde, p. 9; interview, author, Williamson, 22 Jan 93;

AAR, Opn BUSHMASTER I, 3d Bde, 1st Inf Div, an. B, p. 2 (quoted words).

AAR, Opn BUSHMASTER 1, 3d Bde, 1st Inf Div, an. B, p. 2 (quoted words).

Adolf Hitler - https://www.history.com/topics/world-war-ii/adolf-hitler-1

Allied Superiority. https://www.britannica.com/event/World-War-II/Developments-from-summer-1944-to-autumn-1945

Allied Victory over Axis Power Japan. https://www.bbc.co.uk/newsround/33945717

Allied Victory over Axis Powers Germany and Italy. http://www.bbc.co.uk/history/worldwars/wwtwo/how_the_allies_won_01.shtml

Annual Hist Supp, [1965], 2d Bn, 33d Arty, 17 Mar 66. All in box 3, 81/469, RG 338, NARA.

Army S2 officers https://careertrend.com/list-6692783-s2-army-officer-duties.html

Axis Sally. https://www.historynet.com/axis-sally.htm

Battle of France. Blatt, Joel, ed. (1997). *The French Defeat of 1940: Reassessments.* Providence, RI: Berghahn. ISBN 1-57181-109-5.

Battling Buzzards: The Odyssey of the 517th Parachute Regimental Combat Team 1943-1945 Astor, Gerald (1983).

Black Soldier White Army. Bowers, William T. (1996). Center of Military History Pub 70-65 ISBN9781076314284

Bloody Brook, Battle of, Mass., 1675. Massachusetts Historical Society Everett, Edward, 1794-1865. Boston : Russell, Shattuck, & Williams, 1835.

Bob Hope - https://www.uso.org/stories/154-bob-hope-the-uso-s-one-man-morale-machine

Breuer, William B. (1986). *Operation Dragoon*. Presidio Press. ISBN: 0-89141-601-3. p247.

Camp Toccoa: https://www.camptoccoaatcurrahee.org/history-of-camp-toccoa

Churchill by Himself: In His Own Words - 9 October 1948, speech to the Conservative Party Congress at Llandudno, Wales

D-Day, June 6, 1944: The Battle for the Normandy Beaches. Ambrose, Stephen (1997). *London: Simon & Schuster. p. 34. ISBN 0-7434-4974-6.*

DAR Genealogical Research Databases. Daughters of the American Revolution, database online, (http://www.dar.org/ : accessed January 23, 2015), «Record of Benjamin Talmage», Ancestor # A112617.

Darrel Nash, 24th Infantry Regiment Historian

Elements of Command pt. I, p. la, Intel to Interview, Patterson with Seaman, 1971-72;

Field Marshall Montgomery http://www.bbc.co.uk/history/historic_figures/montgomery_bernard.shtml

Fall of Manhay—https://history.army.mil/books/wwii/7-8/7-8_23.HTM

Fighting Power: German and US Army Performance, 1939–1945. Van Creveld, Martin (1982). Westport, Connecticut: Greenwood Press. ISBN 978-0-31309-157-5.

Genealogy of One Line of the Hopkins Family, Descended from Thomas Hopkins in Providence, from 1641 to 1692. Holbrook, Albert. Washington [District of Columbia]

General Dwight D. Eisenhower. https://www.history.com/topics/us-presidents/dwight-d-eisenhower

General Eisenhower 19 December Conference. https://www.historynet.com/untold-story-patton-bastogne.htm

General Eisenhower's J-2: Major General Kenneth Strong, British Army Intelligence. https://www.jstor.org/stable/44326949?seq=1

General George S. Patton Third Army - http://pattonthirdarmy.com/3rdarmysummaries1.html

General Herman Balck - https://militaryhistorynow.com/2019/08/21/meet-hermann-balck-the-trailblazing-panzer-general-that-history-forgot/

General Matthew B. Ridgway: www.goodreads.com/author/quotes/600238.Matthew_B_Ridgway

German Third Reich declaration of war. https://en.wikisource.org/wiki/Adolf_Hitler%27s_Declaration_of_War_against_the_United_States

Gordon's Silver Star award—Military Hall of Honor, LLC (2020). https://militaryhallofhonor.com/honoree-record.php?id=260775

Grace Liner Santa Rosa http://www.oceanlinermuseum.co.uk/Santa_Rosa_1932_History.html

Hitler's Wehrmacht, 1935–1945. Lexington: University Press of Kentucky. ISBN 978-0-81316-738-1. https://www.historynet.com/death-of-the-wehrmacht-1942.htm

Japanese declaration of war. http://tmcdaniel.palmerseminary.edu/Rescript-English.pdf

Jerry Goldsmith. https://www.imdb.com/name/nm0000025/awards?ref_=nm_awd

Largest Tank Battle. https://www.warhistoryonline.com/world-war-ii/battle-of-kursk-tank.html

Lippman Was Lemmon's Hero. https://www.southdakotamagazine.com/lippman-was-lemmons-hero

Major General John Seaman. https://en.wikipedia.org/wiki/Jonathan_O._Seaman

Marshall von Rundstedt - https://www.britannica.com/biography/Gerd-von-Rundstedt

Memoranda Relating to the Ancestry and Family of Hon. Levi Parsons Morton Leach, Josiah Granville. (Riverside Press, Cambridge, 1894)

New Deal. https://www.history.com/topics/great-depression/new-deal

New York Stock Exchange. https://u-s-history.com/pages/h1806. html

Norman Rockwell. https://u-s-history.com/pages/h3805.html

Operation Hump. https://en.wikipedia.org/wiki/Operation_Hump

Operation Bushmaster. https://en.wikipedia.org/wiki/1st_Infantry_ Division_(United_States)#Vietnam

Operation Bushmaster II. https://en.wikipedia.org/wiki/Operation_ Bushmaster_II

Ostlegionen. D-Day, June 6, 1944: The Battle for the Normandy Beaches. Ambrose, Stephen *(1997).* London: Simon & Schuster. *p. 34. ISBN 0-7434-4974-6.*

Paul Harvey (September 4, 1918-February 28, 2009) http://www. paulharveyarchives.com/

PFC Melvin Biddle, Medal of Honor Winner. http://517prct.org/ ArmyValues-excerpt.htm

Presidential Unit Citation. https://en.wikipedia.org/wiki/ Presidential_Unit_Citation_(United_States)

Quarterly CO Rpt, 1 Oct- 31 Dec 65, 1st Inf Div, pp. 9, 12. See also [Annual Hist Rpt, 1965], 1st Bn, 26th Inf, 29 Mar 66; Annual Supp to Unit History, [1965, 1st Bn, 2d lnf, 25 Mar 66;

Report of Visit to 3d Brigade, 1st Infantry Division. Memo, Lt Col Williamson for Chief, ACTIV, 16 Nov 65, sub: pp. 1- 2.

Report of Visit to 3d Brigade, 1st Infantry Division, pp. 1-2, Historians files, CMH Memo, Lt Col Dan H. Williamson, Jr., M113 Project

Officer, for Chief, Army Concept Team in Vietnam (ACTIV), 16 Nov 65, sub.

S3 https://careertrend.com/about-7217244-army-s3-job-description. html

SS Intent, Albright with Seaman, 10 Sep 70, p. 17; Quarterly Cmd Rpt, 1 Oct- 31 Dec 65, 1st Inf Div, p. 7; Seaman, "Elements of Command," pt. I, p. 10, Incl to Interview, Patterson with Seaman, 1971- 72.

Strategic Army Command Parachute Team (STRAC). https://www. goarmy.com/events/golden-knights/history.html

Supreme Headquarters Allied Expeditionary Force (SHAEF) https://en.wikipedia.org/wiki/Supreme_Headquarters_Allied_ Expeditionary_Force/

*The Battle of Ap Bau Bang, 12 November 1965*Press Release, Info Office, 1st Inf Div, 20 Feb 67, sub:, p. 2 (quoted word s), in Vietnam Interview (VNI) 139, CMH.

The Combat Infantryman Badge (CIB) https://www.cibassoc.com/ about/combat-infantryman-badge/

The Greatest Generation. Brokaw, Tom. (Random House, May 2001)

The Medal of Honor <https://www.army.mil/medalofhonor/history. html>

The Distinguished Service Cross (DSC) <https://valor.defense.gov/ Description-of-Awards/>

The Silver Star <https://valor.defense.gov/Description-of-Awards/>

The Bronze Star <https://valor.militarytimes.com/award/7>

The Purple Heart <https://www.military.com/history/military-heroes/purple-heart>

Third Reich - https://www.britannica.com/place/Third-Reich

Thomas Remington of Suffield, Conn., and Some of His Descendants, Dewey, Louis Marinus. The New England Historical & Genealogical Register (NEHGS, Boston, Mass., 1909) Vol. 63

Treasury Secretary Henry Morgenthau. https://u-s-history.com/pages/h1651.html

U.S. War Bonds. https://u-s-history.com/pages/h1682.html

Western Front. MacDonald, C (2005), *The Last Offensive: The European Theater of Operations.* University Press of the Pacific, p.478 Müller, Rolf-Dieter (2016).

Winston Churchill. https://scottmanning.com/content/churchills-battle-of-the-bulge/

With a Black Platoon in Combat. Rishell, Lyle (1993). Texas A&M University Press. p102 ISBN 978-1-60344-740-9

WPA Shutdown. https://www.history.com/topics/great-depression/works-progress-administration

WPA. Works Progress Administration.

ACKNOWLEDGMENTS

THIS BOOK IS DEDICATED TO the men of the following Army combat units that served with Gordon through 11 campaigns, along with their families and their legacies.

517th Parachute Infantry Regiment (WWII)
82nd Airborne Division (WWII)
24th Infantry Regiment (Korea)
34th Infantry Regiment (Korea)
3rd Brigade, 1st Infantry Division (Vietnam)

He learned from some of those men, led some of those men, served the good of this great country with them all, supported others and received support from still others. Gordon learned how to be a good soldier with the 517th at Camp Toccoa and continued to develop his skills and behavior throughout his career.

His fellow soldiers in these units enjoyed mutual benefits, experiencing the "thrill of victory and the agony of defeat" along with Gordon. That reference to ABC's *Wide World of Sports* tag line is appropriate here—not in the sporting context but for the sheer emotional aspect of what these men went through.

Countless millions of American men and women, from colonial times through the twenty-first century and beyond, willingly sacrifice their lives to advance the cause of freedom-loving people all over the globe. We have traveled through time with one such warrior and his fellow troopers.

Thank you to everyone who has assisted me in putting this story on paper. You have helped me put my vision into an educational and readable format with your encouragement, feedback, editing, and prayers—which have helped tremendously!

Thanks to my Lord and Savior, Jesus Christ, for giving me the grit and ability to capture this story, remain determined, and put it down on paper.

Thanks to my family, and especially my wife Patricia, for her immeasurable patience and for being my cheerleader.

To my children, Jon, Tori, and Alex Roman, Gordon and Lucille's children, Lura Lee Weller, Mark Lippman and Mike Lippman, I thank you from the depths of my heart for reading many manuscript editions, providing critical feedback and insight so that this story would be true to the man we love.

Terry Megli, without your specific encouragement to me to sit down and write this book, I would have continued to procrastinate and would have never started writing. Thank you!

To the following, I am greatly indebted:

Gordon and Lucille Lippman, who made all this possible with their love, kindness, humble and steadfast leadership that created the basis for this story.

Special thanks to Mike Lippman, who provided innumerable personal insights, letters, photos, commendations and background stories. He continues to maintain Gordon's legacy today by providing personal artifacts to the Camp Toccoa Museum and maintains Gordon's story on www.togetherweserved.com.

My sisters, Gail Wells and Rae Lynn Vittorino, helped me develop the story so that it flowed chronologically and gave Gordon his due recognition every step of the way.

Cousins Linda Flounders, Charles Boussad and Robert Eggert, for their insight and assistance.

Co-author David Smale helped me polish up the manuscript, edited my grammar and book structure, advised on the story arc, and helped to develop the storyline, then provided guidance based on his vast writing experience to make it ready for publication.

Thank you to Private First-Class George Rumsey, Master Sergeant Willie N. Robinson, Corporal Asia J. Peterson, Lieutenant Lyle Rishell, and Lieutenant Colonel (retired) Jay Franz, contemporaries of Gordon's who knew him, served with him, and offered their personal eyewitness reports of his character, valor, and leadership.

Thanks particularly to Gordon's sister, Marlys Buchenau, for her tireless efforts in promoting Gordon's legacy to the state of South Dakota and anyone else who might listen.

CPSIA information can be obtained
at www.ICGtesting.com
Printed in the USA
LVHW091648011021
699243LV00001B/42